Coordinating
Social Services

Neil Gilbert
Harry Specht

The Praeger Special Studies program—utilizing the most modern and efficient book production techniques and a selective worldwide distribution network—makes available to the academic, government, and business communities significant, timely research in U.S. and international economic, social, and political development.

Coordinating Social Services

An Analysis of Community, Organizational, and Staff Characteristics

PRAEGER SPECIAL STUDIES IN U.S. ECONOMIC, SOCIAL, AND POLITICAL ISSUES

Praeger Publishers New York London

Library of Congress Cataloging in Publication Data

Gilbert, Neil
    Coordinating social services.

    (Praeger special studies in U.S. economic, social,
and political issues)
    Includes bibliographical references.
    1. Social work administration. 2. Community
organization. 3. Social service—United States.
I. Specht, Harry, joint author. II. Title.
HV40.G54   658'.91'361   76–58555
ISBN 0–275–24330–3

PRAEGER PUBLISHERS
200 Park Avenue, New York, N.Y. 10017, U.S.A.

Published in the United States of America in 1977
by Praeger Publishers, Inc.

Printed in the United States of America

ACKNOWLEDGMENTS

This monograph is based on a study funded by the Administration on Aging, Department of Health, Education, and Welfare (Grant No. 90-A-368/01). We wish to thank the Administration on Aging for its support. Mr. David Dowd, of the Administration on Aging, was most helpful in seeing this project through to fruition. We also would like to express our appreciation to Professor Robert Morris of Brandeis University for reviewing and commenting upon an early draft of this study.

CONTENTS

LIST OF TABLES

LIST OF FIGURES

The major objective of Title III, authorized by the Older Americans Comprehensive Services Amendments of 1973,[1] is to strengthen and develop a system of coordinated services for older people at the substate or area level. This program's regulations require that each state divide itself into planning and services areas to develop and implement area plans.[2] On signing that bill into law, the president took note of those features of the legislation that "authorize financial assistance for area-wide planning within individual States, thus opening the way to more comprehensive and coordinated systems for the delivery of services."[3]

The objective of this study is to provide insights into community, organizational, and staff characteristics associated with the coordination of services process. While the study was commissioned by the Administration on Aging to furnish knowledge that would enhance the operational capacity of Area Agencies on Aging, the questions addressed are of fundamental interest to all organizations engaged in planning and coordination of social services. These basic questions concern, for example: (a) the optimum number of agencies to involve in social service coordination projects; (b) the types of local social service agencies that most often participate in coordination projects; (c) the appropriate roles of coordinating agencies at different phases of the project; (d) the relevance of alternative structural arrangements for citizen participation in coordination projects. In efforts to answer these and other central issues in the coordination of social services the study analyzes a broad range of service coordination experience in the Model Cities Program.

Model Cities is a large-scale effort to strengthen the coordination of services for socially and economically deprived neighborhoods in 147 cities. While the objectives and purposes of the Model Cities Program differ somewhat from the objectives of the 1973 amendments to the Older Americans Act, the two programs emphasize attaining substantial levels of coordination among agencies. As with the Model Cities Agency, there are a number of secondary objectives subsumed under the Administration on Aging's coordination objective. These subobjectives include a desire to rationalize planning, to increase efficiency, effectiveness, and responsiveness, to broaden the base of organizational and consumer participation, and to promote comprehensiveness. These objectives are expressed in the Administration on Aging guidelines for area planning, which set forth the following purposes of the Title III program:

> Provide for the development and implementation by the area agency, in conjunction with other planners and services providers, and older consumers of services, of an area plan which sets forth specific program objectives and priorities. . . .

Increase the capability of the area agency to develop and implement action programs designed to achieve the coordination of existing social service systems in order to make such systems more effective, efficient, and responsive in meeting the needs of the elderly. . . .

Draw in increasing commitments from public and private agencies which have resources that can be utilized to serve older persons and encourage such agencies to enter into cooperative arrangements. . . .

Promote comprehensive services for the elderly. . . .[4]

Similar objectives were operative in the Model Cities Program, which we shall describe in Chapter 1. As we shall make clear in Chapter 4, all of these objectives are not complementary and some of them may, in fact, conflict with one another. By examining the Model Cities experiences we hope to illuminate some of the relationships among variables affecting coordination that are characteristic of coordination efforts in general.

Study Framework

In its most general form, the problem addressed in this study may be expressed briefly as follows: Under what conditions are coordination-of-service efforts likely to be most successful? In the framework used to study this problem we have divided conditions potentially related to coordination efforts into three categories: community context; organizational characteristics; and staff characteristics. Specifically, the following variables are analyzed in each category:

Community context: These contextual variables include basic characteristics of the community and of the planning processes that preceded the coordination effort.

1. community size
2. ethnic composition
3. involvement and support of local chief executive
4. degree of citizen participation in planning
5. structure of citizen participation arrangement
6. degree of conflict experienced during planning
7. previous community experience with large-scale coordination efforts

Organizational characteristics: These variables focus upon the numbers, types, and degrees of commitment of participating agencies in the coordination efforts.

1. number of agencies participating in planning
2. number of agencies that participated in the coordination effort

3. types of agencies involved in coordination, such as: welfare agencies, chamber of commerce, health agencies, colleges, and public housing
4. degree of financial commitment of participating agencies
5. types of agencies most or least likely to provide financial aid
6. size of the coordinating agency

Staff characteristics: The variables in this category relate to the roles, functions, and experience of coordinating agency staff.

1. professionalization of coordinating agencies
2. professional background of agency directors
3. degree of normative authority exercised by the directors
4. director turnover
5. director emphasis upon process or task functions
6. staff roles

The contextual, organizational, and staff characteristics outlined above are the major independent variables in this study. The major dependent variable is "success of coordination." This is a composite measure based on interview ratings of federal officials and analysis of regional evaluation documents.

OVERVIEW

In Chapter 1 the setting for this study is described. This section presents a brief review of the background of the Model Cities Program and explains how it operates.

As is often the case in social research on action programs, many of the variables in this study that appeared to be important and interesting (for example, citizen influence, conflict, agency support, coordination success) were also extremely complex and difficult to measure in quantitative form. In Chapter 2 we provide a detailed explanation of the data collection methods and operational definitions of variables used in this study.

The relationships between the outcomes of coordination efforts and the contextual and organizational characteristics of planning and implementation are analyzed in Chapters 3 and 4 respectively; and relationships between coordination efforts and staff characteristics are analyzed in Chapter 5. In Chapters 3, 4, and 5 the empirical evidence of the coordination experiences of the Model Cities is examined in light of theoretical and empirical work found in the literature on service coordination. Where relevant, specific propositions derived from this literature are compared with our findings.

The main focus of the study is upon conditions related to "success of coordination." This dependent variable refers to the degree to which programs were judged able to *implement the coordination process* (for example, meshing complementary activities and joint planning). It does not evaluate the coordination process with reference to the programs that were ultimately produced. For example, we do not assess the effectiveness and efficiency of service-delivery efforts that developed as a result of the coordination efforts. However, although the study data do not include program effectiveness and program efficiency measures, there are two general measures used to assess these aspects of program implementation: (1) service-delivery output as a function of the proportion of allocated funds spent in the first year of program; and (2) ratings of overall first-year program achievements. In Chapter 6 the coordination-of-service effort is analyzed as an independent variable in relation to these measures of implementation. That is, in Chapters 3, 4, and 5 we analyze the factors that are associated with the implementation of the coordination process, and in Chapter 6 we assess how coordination outcomes are associated with other measures of program implementation.

In Chapters 3, 4, 5, and 6 the general approach taken is to examine the degree to which implementation of the coordination effort is associated with different variables. Here the analysis of the data usually involves the use of percentages in contingency tables and statistical measures of association between coordination and the other study variables. In Chapter 7 a more complex mode of analysis is applied to the data. Selecting the variables that seem most strongly associated with coordination efforts, we attempt to develop an exploratory model that combines these relevant variables and indicates which are the best predictors of successful coordination when the effects of the others are held constant. Finally, in Chapter 8 we examine the implications for practice suggested by some of the main findings.

NOTES

1. S. 50, Public Law 93–29, approved May 3, 1973.
2. *Washington Social Legislation Bulletin,* 23:21; November 12, 1973, p. 83.
3. *Weekly Compilation of Presidential Documents* 9 (1973): 450–51
4. U.S. Department of Health, Education, and Welfare, *Area Plan for Programs on Aging under Title III of the Older Americans Act of 1965 As Amended* (Washington, D.C.: Government Printing Office, October 1973), Section B, pp. 1–2.

Coordinating
Social Services

1

In the 1960s, community planning for local service-delivery systems was transformed. Three main factors contributed to this transformation. The first was the citizen participation movement, with its roots in civil rights efforts, the planning programs spawned by the President's Committee on Juvenile Delinquency, and the Economic Opportunity Program of 1964. Historically, community planning and decision making in social welfare had been the almost-exclusive province of traditional agencies and professional groups of the kind that constituted the membership of community health and welfare councils. Through the citizen participation movement, decision making for planning service-delivery systems was broadened to include many more segments of the community, especially representatives of client groups and residents of low-income neighborhoods. The second factor contributing to the transformation of community planning was the increasing involvement of public agencies and city governments in planning for the delivery of social welfare services. Hitherto, social welfare planning had been relegated primarily to the private/voluntary planning efforts of local health and welfare councils. The third factor was the introduction of procedures to expedite the coordination of national grant-in-aid programs at the local level.

EMERGING EMPHASIS ON COORDINATION

The coordination of local services gained special prominence in the Economic Opportunity Program initiated in 1964. One of the reasons why coordinating activities were accentuated in the mid-1960s was the tremendous expansion in the number and size of the federal grant-in-aid programs during this period. Between 1962 and 1966 it is estimated that the number of federal categorical-grant programs increased from 160 to 349, and by 1971 there were more than 500. In 1971, close to three quarters of the 30 billion dollars that the federal government allocated to smaller units of government was for human-service types of programs.[1]

So many local private, quasi-public, and public organizations received various federal grants for provision of various kinds of services that large-city mayors found it difficult even to keep abreast of the amounts, locations, and purposes of these grants. The coordination of a city's social welfare-related activities involves not only different types and large numbers of organizations, but also the crossing of the jurisdictional lines of different public bodies. For example, a city might get services from a county public health department, a state department of public assistance, a state agency for unemployment compensation, and a local board of education that is either elected or appointed and has its own taxing power. Many antipoverty agencies were created as private nonprofit corporations rather than as units of city government because it was thought that if they were established as city agencies, these efforts to coordinate interjurisdictional public bodies would be likely to encounter stiff resistance.[2] On the whole, though, disengagement of antipoverty agencies from city hall did not enhance coordinative efforts. In many cases, the struggles that erupted between city hall and antipoverty agencies diminished the capacity of both sides to coordinate services. Available evidence suggests that coordination in the antipoverty program achieved limited results.[3]

Following the antipoverty program, federally initiated efforts to improve planning and coordination of service-delivery systems in the 1960s culminated in the Model Cities Program. The lessons of the antipoverty program and other previous efforts at urban improvement and human resource development were useful to planners of the Model Cities Program, even where results were considerably different from those anticipated. As Fred Jordan observes:

> That those lessons were, more frequently than not, instructive of what not to do rather than what to do did not lessen their value for the group of men and women who were planning the program, working for passage of enabling legislation, and thereafter erecting the policy framework that would give it life and substance.[4]

THE MODEL CITIES PROGRAM

The Model Cities Program, framed in the enabling legislation—Title I of the Demonstration Cities and Metropolitan Development Act of 1966 (P. L. 89–754)—is one of the most substantial ventures in community planning yet initiated by the federal government. The program emphasized a comprehensive, coordinated approach to local planning that would attack the problems of urban decay and human strife affecting large sections of cities throughout the nation. A comprehensive coordinated approach is described in the *Program Guide* of the Department of Housing and Urban Development (HUD) as including physical improvement, housing, transportation, education, manpower and economic development, recreation and culture, crime reduction, health, social services, and public assistance—although this list was to be considered "neither exhaustive nor directive."[5]

Briefly, the Model Cities Program was run in the following way. All cities were invited by HUD to submit applications for planning grants. In these applications the cities described their characteristics, their social problems, and their "plan for planning." In the first application period, which ended May 1, 1967, 193 cities had sent in applications. After a careful and complex scrutiny of the applications and the applicants, 75 cities were selected to receive planning grants.[6] Announcement of the grants was made on November 16, 1967. A similar process was used in the following year to select another 73 cities. (One of the cities originally selected dropped out at an early stage, bringing the total to 147 program participants.) The cities and towns chosen had populations ranging in size from approximately 2,000 to 8 million.

Participation in the Model Cities Program was expected to last approximately six years. The first year was to be devoted to planning, the product of which was a document called the "Comprehensive Demonstration Plan" (CDP). The CDP was to describe the content and objectives of program components to be implemented in the following program year, to specify the administrative arrangements for coordination of these program components, and to set the general framework for programs over a continuing five-year period.[7]

A City Demonstration Agency (CDA) was organized in each of the Model Cities to do the job of planning and coordinating the program. At the conclusion of the period of planning, which might have lasted anywhere from ten months to two years, the CDAs submitted their CDPs to HUD for review and funding.

HUD grants to Model Cities Programs were called "supplemental funds." These are similar to block grants and could be used flexibly to support a variety of Model Cities projects. Under the Model Cities statute, supplemental funds were to be used "to assist new and additional projects and activities not assisted under a Federal grant-in-aid program. To the extent such funds are not necessary to support fully such new and additional projects and activities, they may be used and credited as part or all of the required non-Federal contribution to projects or activities, assisted in a Federal grant-in-aid program, which are part of an approved comprehensive city demonstration program."[8] One major objective of the use of supplemental funds was to provide some leverage for the coordination of existing federal programs that might be related to the Model Cities effort.[9]

This study focuses upon the coordination experiences and the conditions associated with these experiences in the Model Cities Program from the initial selection of applicants in November 1967 to the spring of 1971. This period covers the planning year and some part of the first program year for all participating cities. Specifically, by spring 1971 approximately 117 cities had completed at least six months of their first program year and 65 had completed the entire twelve months of their first program year.

NOTES

1. Edward Banfield, "Revenue Sharing in Theory and Practice," *Public Interest* 23 (Spring 1971): 33–44.
2. Neil Gilbert, *Clients or Constituents* (San Francisco: Jossey Bass, 1970), pp. 52–53.
3. Edward J. O'Donnell and Marilyn Sullivan, "Service Delivery and Social Action through the Neighborhood Center: A Review of Research," *Welfare in Review* (November/December 1969): 1–2; Ralph Kramer, *Participation of the Poor* (Englewood Cliffs: Prentice-Hall, 1969); Neil Gilbert, "Neighborhood Coordinator: Advocate or Middleman?" *Social Service Review* 43 (June 1969): 136–44.
4. Fred Jordan, "Model Cities in Perspective: A Selective History," in *Model Cities: A Report on Progress, Special Issue of the Model Cities Service Center Bulletin* (Washington, D. C.: Government Printing Office, 1971), p. 4.
5. U.S. Department of Housing and Urban Development, *Improving the Quality of Urban Life: A Program Guide to Model Neighborhoods in Demonstration Cities* (Washington, D. C.: Government Printing Office, 1966), p. 47.
6. For a detailed description and analysis of this selection process, see Neil Gilbert and Harry Specht, " 'Picking Winners': Federal Discretion and Local Experiences as Bases for Planning Grant Allocations," *Public Administration Review* 34 (November/December 1974): 565–74.
7. For further details on the Model Cities Program legislation, guidelines, and operational procedures, see the following: U.S. Department of Housing and Urban Development, *Improving the Quality of Urban Life: A Program Guide to Model Neighborhoods in Demonstration Cities* (Washington, D. C.: Government Printing Office, HUD PG-47, December 1966, and HUD PG-47, December 1967); Marshall Kaplan, *Model Cities and National Urban Policy* (Chicago: American Society of Planning Officials, 1971); *The Model Cities Program* (Washington, D. C.: Government Printing Office, 1970); and Roland Warren, "Model Cities First Round: Politics, Planning, and Participation," *Journal of the American Institute of Planners* 34 (July 1969): 245–52.
8. U.S. Congress, *Demonstration Cities and Metropolitan Development Act 1966*, Public Law 89–754, Section 105 (d).
9. For further details on the uses of supplemental funds, see U.S. Department of Housing and Urban Development, *The Federal Grant Process: An Analysis of the Use of Supplemental and Categorical Funds in the Model Cities Program* (Washington, D. C.: Government Printing Office, 1972).

2

STUDY METHODOLOGY

The data upon which our study is based were obtained by different methods from various sources, including structured interviews with upper-echelon HUD officials; a questionnaire survey of all CDAs; and content analyses of HUD documents and reports that were made on each city. Where it was necessary to transform qualitative judgments into quantitative form we attempted to obtain data for these judgments from at least two independent sources in order to increase the confidence in our measures. These efforts notwithstanding, our indicators are, at best, approximations of the subtle and complex phenomena with which the study deals. To some extent we have sacrificed the in-depth detail of the case study approach to obtain the broader view of the population survey. There are, of course, benefits and disadvantages to both approaches. The case study is limited in the amount of social terrain that can be covered (usually a few cases), but puts the investigator closer to the reality of the terrain that is within his purview. The survey approach tends to put the investigator farther from the reality under investigation, but allows for the inclusion of many cases and, therefore, offers opportunity for comparative analysis.

How well our indicators reflect the reality we are seeking to comprehend is, ultimately, for the reader to decide. We will describe in detail the sources of data and how our indicators were operationally defined.

SOURCES OF DATA

Interviews

Structured interviews were conducted with 11 HUD officials in Washington, D.C. (most of whom were known in the bureaucratic jargon as "deskmen") who were responsible for managing and maintaining relationships with city and regional staff. Each of these officials had direct responsibility for programs in from 12 to 30 cities within a region; taken together these officials had covered all of the first- and second-round programs over the planning year and into the first action year. At the time of the interviews (August 1971), some of these officials had moved to other positions within HUD or to other programs.

Each interviewee was asked to make a comparative rating of the Model Cities Programs under their jurisdiction for 17 variables, including degree of citizen influence; support of the chief executive; role of CDA directors; and success of coordination efforts. Most of the ratings were made along a five-point continuum ranging from "weakest" to "strongest," "least" to "most," and the like.

These interviews averaged two hours and both authors were present, except for a few cases where scheduling required that two respondents be interviewed at the same time. The officials interviewed were cooperative in giving both their time and their thought to our project. They expressed virtually no reservations in talking about the Model Cities Program experiences or in making comparative judgments about the programs that were under their jurisdictions. As some of the respondents indicated, this high degree of cooperation was due, in part, to the fact that by the summer of 1971 federal interest in the Model Cities Program had diminished considerably; revenue sharing was on the horizon, and it appeared to HUD officials that the program would probably be phased out in the not-too-distant future. Moreover, by 1971 the Model Cities Program had lost much of its controversy. Thus, the respondents felt quite free to express their opinions about the program experience and the knowledge gained therein. And they seemed pleased that an attempt was being made to record this experience and knowledge from their perspective.

While unable to insure the accuracy of respondents' recall, we were able to obtain additional data from narrative documents written on each program about the events under consideration in the interviews, at the time these events took place. Where possible, these additional data provided a second set of ratings that were incorporated in the final operational definitions of the study variables.

Documents

The major documentary sources that were drawn upon for analysis in this study were narrative reports written by HUD regional staff (known as "leadmen"). The leadmen were responsible for monitoring and providing various forms of assistance to the programs in their regions. As part of their monitoring activities these regional staff prepared briefing memos and quarterly reports

on each program under their jurisdictions, which were forwarded to the deskmen at HUD in Washington, D.C. The briefing memos were summary reports
written at the end of the planning year and the first action year. These documents described each city's experience in terms of progress made, obstacles
encountered, and general program strengths and weaknesses. Three of the
main subheadings of these reports referred to coordination and utilization of
resources; administrative capability and local commitment; and community
participation. For example, accounts of citizen participation in two programs
were given as follows:

> City A: The plan was basically developed by CDA and agency staff. The
> four Model Area Planning councils participated actively in the problem
> analysis but after that their role was primarily one of reacting to City
> proposals.
>
> [Excerpted from Chicago Briefing Memo]
>
> City B: The City-citizen relationship can be characterized as a partnership
> in which the citizens have an active, initiating, strong role. The citizens have
> an important part to play; but it is still a partnership, completely dependent
> on active City support in formulating and implementing plans. Thus far, the
> partnership appears to be a success.
>
> [Excerpted from Cambridge Briefing Memo]

The quarterly reports are narrative records of program progress during
the first action year, similar to the briefing memos, but prepared on a quarterly
basis. Quarterly reports were used to obtain data in the cases where the briefing
memos were not available, usually because these programs were funded in the
second round (between November 1968 and early 1969) and had not completed their first action year at the time of the study.

A content analysis of these documents was done using three readers who
independently rated each program for degree of citizen participation in planning, chief executive support, and implementation of citizen participation and
success of coordination in the first action year. The ratings were made along
a three-point continuum based on sets of descriptions of behaviors that characterized each point. (These descriptions of variables were the same as those used
to elicit deskmen's responses to the interview questions.) Ratings given these
variables for each program were accepted if at least two readers were in
agreement; otherwise the rating was discarded and no score given that variable
for the program on which agreement was not reached.

In addition to the above sources, information on each program's budget
expenditures (for supplemental funds) in the first action year was provided by
the HUD accounting office. Data on previous experience in urban renewal and
public housing programs were obtained from the *Urban Renewal Directory,
1967* and the *Consolidated Development Directory, 1967.*

Survey

We conducted a mail survey of all 147 programs, under the sponsorship of the U.S. Conference of Mayors. A questionnaire addressed to CDA directors was sent to the 147 programs and the rate of return was 76 percent.

The questionnaire asked about: (a) the professional and educational background of CDA directors and staff; (b) size and ethnic composition of the Model Neighborhood Area or MNA (target neighborhood); (c) the structural relationships of resident-organization staff to the CDA; (d) the roles of CDA director and staff; (e) the number and kinds of public and private agencies participating in the program and the continuity of their participation from the planning year to the first action year; and (f) a breakdown of the CDA budget for the first action year in terms of the percent of funds from supplemental, categorical, and other sources, and the agencies contributing these funds. A copy of the survey questionnaire is in the Appendix.

Finally, a measure of turbulence/conflict for 1967–68 was obtained from data on a nationwide survey done by the Lemberg Center for the Study of Violence, Brandeis University, which the center made available for our use.[1]

OPERATIONAL DEFINITIONS

The measurement of some of the variables used in this study involved subjective ratings of units of analysis that are not very concrete, such as *success of coordination efforts; degree of citizen participation; degree of conflict* in planning; and *degree of chief executive support.* For these variables, indicators were developed from qualitative judgments that were quantified along an ordinal scale. These judgments were obtained by the two methods previously described: content analysis of HUD documents prepared by regional staff (leadmen) and structured interviews with HUD officials in Washington, D.C. (deskmen). Thus it should be noted that these indicators represent a "federal perspective" on what was happening in the Model Cities Program. In many respects this perspective probably allows for as clear a view of the Model Cities Program nationwide as could be hoped for. These informants were close enough to a number of programs for a long enough period of time to be able to make informed comparative judgments (as compared, for example, to local CDA staff or citizen participants who knew only their own city's programs); yet they were removed enough from these programs to allow their judgments to be made with a reasonable degree of objectivity (as compared to local staff or citizen participants whose investments in their own programs might color their views).

In addition, it should be noted that the two sets of judgments derived from the federal perspective, strictly speaking, are not totally independent. Originally the briefing memos were prepared by regional HUD staff as reports for consumption by the Washington deskmen. Hence the views of the Washington officials we interviewed were formed partly out of the information received in these reports as well as through their direct contact with the programs. We expected that these two sets of judgments would show a high degree of consistency. Based on these judgments the four qualitative variables noted above were operationally defined and constructed as follows.

Citizen influence in the planning process: In developing this indicator we asked HUD officials to rate each of the programs under their jurisdiction along a five-point continuum of citizen influence on decision making as it appeared during the last quarter of the planning period. This time frame was chosen because it was during the last quarter of the planning year that decision making for the Comprehensive Development Plan concentrated on the actual program proposals for the first action year. Also, focusing on the last quarter allowed for the fact that citizen participation often varied over the planning year and accurate generalizations about the entire period would be more difficult to make than generalizations about a strategic quarter. Finally, we had access to other data which focused mainly on this last quarter and which could be compared with the deskmen's ratings. As bases for rating judgments, criteria were provided for the extremes and the midpoint of the rating continuum. The descriptions were given as follows:

Weak citizen influence (staff influence is the major determinant in decision making)—MNA residents functioned primarily to legitimize the planning processes and products originated by the CDA staff. At this end of the continuum, residents play a residual role in decisions and generally rubber-stamp the decisions of CDA staff.

Moderate citizen influence (parity relationship between resident groups and CDA staff)—MNA residents and CDA staff shared responsibility for key planning decisions. At this midpoint on the continuum, residents and staff could be characterized as "equal partners" in the planning enterprise.

Strong citizen influence (resident influence is the major determinant in decision making)—MNA residents exerted preponderant influence in the planning process. At this end of the continuum, residents could be characterized as directors of the planning process.

A second set of ratings on the degree of citizen influence was obtained through the content analysis of briefing memos on each program. Here each program was rated along a three-point continuum, also based upon the above criteria. The two sets of rating judgments (deskmen interviews and content analysis of briefing memos) were correlated and demonstrated a high degree of association (gamma .667). The interview ratings were then collapsed into a three-point continuum (1,2 = weak; 3 = moderate; and 4,5 = strong) and again correlated with the content analysis ratings of briefing memos. This time the degree of association between the two sets of judgments was very strong (gamma .769). We selected the collapsed interview ratings as our indicators of citizen influence in the planning process.

Chief executive support: A procedure similar to that described above was used to obtain measures of chief executive support. HUD officials were asked to rate the programs under their jurisdictions along a five-point continuum. Rating criteria were discussed and general descriptions for the two ends and the midpoint of the continuum were given as follows:

Limited support—Executive's support was primarily "lip service"; little action was taken on the program's behalf without much prodding.

Moderate support—Executive was positively associated with the program to the extent that he could be called upon to act on the program's behalf and frequently produced the desired result.

Active support—Executive was clearly identified as the program's backer; he acted not only on request, but frequently took the initiative in interventions with HUD and local agencies.

Content analysis of the briefing memos produced a second set of ratings on chief executive support along a three-point continuum based upon the above criteria. Correlations between ratings from the interviews and the content analysis showed a moderate degree of association (gamma .470). The two sets of ratings were combined in an index that produced a strong degree of association when correlated independently with each set of ratings (gamma .939 and gamma .734). This index was used as our indicator of chief executive support.

MNA conflict: The HUD officials interviewed were asked to rate the cities under their jurisdiction in terms of the degree of conflict that accompanied the development of the MNA citizen participation structure. A low degree of conflict was described as involving virtually no contest for leadership and jurisdiction among residents in the development of the MNA citizen participation structure. Moderate conflict involved genuine contests for leadership among individuals and groups in the MNA; elections held in these situations were lively, but did not provoke intense feelings. High conflict situations were those in which the struggle for leadership was heated and intense. Sufficient information on this variable was not found in the briefing memos to allow for comparative ratings to be made through the content analysis. Therefore the indicators of MNA conflict in the development of citizen participation structures were based exclusively on the interview ratings.

However, we did have an indicator of community turbulence/conflict during the planning years (1967–68) based on the data from the Lemberg Center for the Study of Violence, Brandeis University. This second set of data was somewhat different from our indicator of MNA conflict. These data focused on reported incidents of disorder for entire cities rather than MNAs, and the disorders reported were more extreme forms of social conflict than were usually manifest in struggles for MNA leadership. Although the indica-

tors of MNA conflict and community turbulence/conflict were not directly
comparable, it was expected that there would be a measure of correspondence
between the degree of conflict in the larger community and that which emerged
in the Model Cities target neighborhood. Correlation between these two indicators showed a strong degree of association (gamma .618). In the absence
of more comparable data against which the subjective interview ratings might
have been matched, this relationship lends some confidence to the accuracy of
the MNA conflict indicator.

   Success of coordination efforts during the first program year: The indicator
of this variable was developed using the same procedure as above. HUD
officials were asked to rate programs according to the degree of interagency
coordination that was achieved during the first program year. The operational
definition given to these officials in the interview was as follows: By successful
coordination we refer to the degree to which a Model Cities Program was
instrumental in pulling together the planning and operation of federally, state,
and locally funded agencies as reflected by the extent to which these programs
were able to eliminate duplication of service efforts and mesh complementary
activities of agencies through, for example, exchange of resources, joint planning, and joint decision-making procedures. A second set of coordination
ratings was obtained through content analysis of federal reports (specifically
the sections of briefing memos that dealt with coordination and utilization of
resources). An index, constructed by combining the two rating sets, produced
a high degree of association when correlated independently with each set
(gammas of .965 and .612). This index represents our indicator of the success
of coordination for each city during the program year.*

   Out of the 147 cities participating in the Model Cities Program, we were
able to construct this index for 68. The missing data mainly reflect the fact that
judgments about the implementation of coordination could not be made for
many cities because more than half of the participating cities had not completed their first program year at the time of the study. Of the 68 cities that
received two consistent ratings on coordination, all except one had been operating projects at least six months into the first program year.

   The operational definitions of the other variables that are analyzed in this
study, such as community size, number of agencies involved in planning,

---

   *The operational definition of coordination used in this study emphasizes basically cooper-
ative processes of exchange. When social planners speak of coordination this view is the one that
most often comes to mind. We might note, however, that there is another way to conceptualize
coordination as a process of adjustments achieved through contest in the interorganizational field.
That view is not examined in this study, although it offers a valid description of how coordination
might occur under certain circumstances. For an analysis of coordination through contest see
Roland Warren et al., *The Structure of Urban Reform* (Lexington, Mass.: Lexington Books, 1974).

ethnic composition, and the like, are relatively self-evident. Data on these variables were collected primarily through the questionnaire survey previously described. Operational measures of the roles played by the agency director and staff are based on self-ratings in the questionnaire responses.

ANALYTIC METHODS

The relationships among variables in this study will be analyzed in two basic forms: by percentages in contingency tables and by a statistical measure of association known as "gamma." The objective of both methods is to summarize large bodies of data for ease of understanding and interpretation.

Percentages simplify descriptions of relationships among variables by equalizing the bases (to 100) upon which variable scores are calculated. This allows us to compare relative differences among the units being examined. When percentages are used in contingency tables they will be calculated in the direction of the variable that is antecedent to other variables or, if the time sequence between variables is indeterminate, in the direction of the variable that is considered to be the influencing factor in the relationship under examination.

"Gamma" is a measure of association between variables that form ordinal scales (ranked high to low, weak to strong, and so on), the form in which most of the data will be presented.[2] Gamma tells us the degree to which a Model Cities Program rank or rating on one variable is predictable from its rank on another. The predictions can be made in two directions: toward perfect agreement among rankings (gamma +1.00) and toward perfect disagreement (gamma −1.00). Agreement indicates that a city ranking high on one variable also ranks high on the other. Disagreement indicates that a city ranking high on one variable ranks low on the other. Technically, a gamma of .589, for example, indicates that there is 58.9 percent greater agreement than disagreement between a city's rank on two variables.

Because the gamma coefficients reflect the general tendency toward linear relationships, a very low gamma value does not eliminate the possibility that a curvilinear relationship (in the form of parabola) might exist among the variables under investigation. Thus, in presenting our findings we will examine the distributions in contingency tables to assess the existence of this nonlinear type of relationship.

Although our data are drawn from the survey of an entire population (rather than from a random sample), the analysis includes measures of the statistical significance (chi-square) of the findings. In this instance significance levels are not used for purposes of generalizing to a population, but as estimates of the extent to which the observed association would be likely to occur by randomly pairing the values of variables under examination.[3]

Finally, in addition to the basic analytic techniques described above, we use multiple regression analysis on an exploratory basis to examine the relationships between specified independent and dependent variables controlling for the effects of other variables in the system. While we will also employ some multivariate analysis using gamma coefficients, this approach is limited because the introduction of a single control variable substantially reduces the cell frequencies in the accompanying tables. The objective here is to explore how theoretical models suggested by the propositions from a series of zero order correlations coincide with the data when analyzed by more powerful techniques. The major problem in using this analytic technique is that we violate some of the assumptions on which regression analysis is based: specifically, in some cases we treat ordinal data as interval data. (Some of our ordinal scales were constructed by collapsing interval data and in these cases we use the raw data scores for the regression analysis.) Also we are dealing with a relatively small n for this type of analysis. Thus, any models that we develop using this technique are highly tentative and mainly of heuristic value.

NOTES

1. For a description of the Lemberg Center survey see Jane Boskin et al., *Race Related Civil Disorders 1967–1969* (Waltham, Massachusetts: Report No. 1, Lemberg Center for the Study of Violence, 1971).

2. The Berkeley Transposed Tab Statistical System was used for computations. The technical details on computation of ordinal measures of association may be found in a number of basic texts and articles. For example, see Linton C. Freeman, *Elementary Applied Statistics* (New York: John Wiley, 1968), and Leo Goodman and William Kruskal, "Measures of Association for Cross Classification," *Journal of the American Statistical Association* 49 (1954): 732–64.

3. For additional discussion of this use of tests of significance see David Gold, "Statistical Tests and Substantive Significance," *The American Sociologist* (February 1969): 42–46.

CHAPTER

3

COMMUNITY CONTEXT

Service-coordination projects are initiated through a planning process that takes place in a community setting. Our "contextual variables" refer to aspects of this process and its setting. The contextual factors contribute to the development of a climate and a structure for the implementation of service-coordination efforts.

There is no grand theory regarding the relative importance of different contextual variables and their relationships to coordination. Instead, the theory and research in this area approach the issue from varying perspectives. Rather than a coherent theory, what emerges from the literature is a series of propositions that emphasize different characteristics of the community context and their potential influence upon service-coordination efforts. Some of these propositions will be examined in this chapter as we analyze the relationships between the implementation of service-coordination efforts and seven relevant characteristics of community context discussed in the literature. The chapter is divided into two parts: the first part deals with demographic variables in the community setting and the second part focuses upon characteristics of the community planning processes.

COMMUNITY SETTING

Community size, planning experience, and proportions of racial minorities in the population are demographic properties of the community that were assessed to determine their potential impact on service-coordination projects. While community size is often selected as a contextual variable in analyses of policy implementation, it is rarely inferred that implementation is directly a function of such a global property as community size.[1] Different theories are found in the literature to explain why large cities are either more likely or less likely to achieve high levels of performance in program implementation. These explanations usually introduce intervening variables associated with size that might account for relationships with programmatic outcomes. The literature suggests two opposing propositions concerning the impact of community size on the implementation of service-coordination projects. First, the negative proposition (that size will be inversely associated with the success of coordination efforts) may be derived from Dye's comparative analysis of the implementation of desegregation policy in 51 cities.[2] Dye finds that large cities were less successful than small cities in implementing desegregation policy. He explains the findings, in part, by the fact that larger cities tend to be more bureaucratic than smaller cities. Theoretically, this point of view assumes that the greater complexity and structural differentiation of larger cities lead to more bureaucratized arrangements, the general inflexibility of which are obstacles to the implementation of new policies. From this perspective, bureaucratization is the intervening variable that explains the negative impact of city size on program implementation. While Dye's study concerned desegregation policy, the theoretical relationships among city size, bureaucratization, and program implementation would seem to apply equally well to implementation of service-coordination projects.

The second proposition (that size will be positively associated with the success of coordination efforts) is supported by studies of Aiken and Alford on the implementation of public housing and urban renewal programs.[3] Their studies reveal strong positive correlations between city size and program implementation. Their findings are explained thus:

> First, larger cities are likely to have more organizations devoted to specific kinds of decision-areas—i.e., more likely to have a redevelopment agency, a housing agency, a community action agency. .... Such organizations are likely to have larger, more specialized, and more professional staffs to provide the technical, administrative, and political knowledge required to innovate successfully, not only within their organizations, but also in the activation of inter-organizational relationships and establishment of critical coalitions. Secondly, it is precisely in the larger, more structurally differentiated communities that coalitions that can implement an innovation will be easiest to establish. If we assume that only a limited number of organizational units need to be mobilized to bring about a successful innovation, then it follows that in large, highly differentiated communities a lower proportion of the available organizations will participate in such decisions, and that there will be wider latitude in selecting organizations for these critical coalitions.[4]

To summarize, the issue is whether the greater bureaucratization that accompanies structural differentiation in large cities is an obstacle to implementation of service-coordination projects because the various bureaucracies tend to develop domain consensus and to become firmly set in their ways; or whether differentiation is an asset because the more bureaucracies (that is, centers of influence) available, the smaller the proportion of the overall system that is required to obtain a critical mass of support for coordination projects. In addition, it is suggested that large cities will possess a greater pool of experience and expertise to implement service-coordination projects than small cities.

The Model Cities data suggest that in regard to success of service coordination, the medium-sized cities appear to have the best overall records. Specifically, the medium-sized cities range in population from 50,000 to 249,999, with the six cities in this group that were rated high on success of coordination clustered around 100,000 to 150,000 in size. Thus, while the entire group of Model Cities ranges in size from a few thousand to over 8 million, a little more than half of the cities rated high on coordination success fell into the 100,000 to 149,999 group. In Table 3.1 we have presented the population categories showing the high success rate of cities in the 100,000 to 149,999 population range. It can be seen that 60 percent of the cities in this population range achieved high ratings on their coordination efforts compared to only 9.4 percent of cities below that range and 7.7 percent of cities above that range.

A tentative explanation for this finding lies in the fact that cities in the 100,000 to 149,999 range of size are large enough to contain a substantial number and variety of service agencies as well as a pool of the skilled and experienced personnel necessary to construct a service-coordination system; yet they are small enough to allow for development of a network of informal relationships among the various agencies and between agencies and city government, a network that facilitates the implementation of coordination efforts. In comparison, small towns (10,000-30,000) that would possess the network of informal relationships usually do not command the required level of agency resources and staff skills. And while the very large cities usually have an abundance of agency resources and professional personnel, the network of relationships among agencies and between agencies and government is difficult to establish because there are more layers of bureaucracy to go through. Accordingly, it would follow that with regard to community size, obstacles to service-coordination efforts are more likely to be experienced in both very large and very small communities than in middle-sized communities. Large cities appear to present the greatest obstacles to coordination efforts, as we will see in Chapter 6, where a more stringent criterion of coordination success is applied, and in Chapter 7, where a more refined analysis is conducted of the relationships between community size (using the interval data on city size rather than ordinal data in grouped categories) and intervening variables that affect the success of coordination.

Table 3.1
Community Size and Success in Coordination
(in percent)

Degree of Success	Community Size		
	Less than 100,000	100,000 to 149,999	More than 149,999
Low	31.2	10	23.1
Moderate	59.4	30	69.2
High	9.4	60	7.7
	100	100	100
	(N=32)	(N=10)	(N=26)

Notes: gamma .105,X^2 = 13.043;Df = 4;p < .02.
Source: All tabular matter in this book was prepared by the authors.

Another property that may affect implementation of service-coordination projects is the community's general capacity in the area of program development. As previously suggested, one of the intervening variables in relationships between city size and program implementation is the large city's presumably greater accumulation of relevant knowledge and experience. In their studies of the implementation of urban renewal and public housing programs Aiken and Alford suggest that the accumulation of planning-related knowledge may be inferred from the city's age. As they explain:

> Presumably older cities have had a longer time for existing organizations to have worked out patterns of interaction, alliances, factions, or coalitions. In such communities the state of knowledge in the community system about the orientations, needs, and probable reactions to varying proposals for community action is likely to be quite high, thus increasing the probability of developing a sufficiently high level of coordination in order to implement successfully a community innovation.[5]

In our analysis of the Model Cities Program (which is of relatively recent origin compared to public housing and urban renewal), rather than using a city's age as an indicator of knowledge and experience accumulated in program development, we employ what would seem to be a more direct measure: the length of the city's prior experience in a relevant program area, specifically, urban renewal. The selection of this indicator takes into account that in the last two decades cities have used urban renewal programs not only to secure federal funds for themselves but also to create, outside the city's regular departmental structure, a cadre of professional talent possessing the knowledge and skills that could be employed in various program development projects. "The best local renewal authorities," Wilson observes, "became generalized sources of innovation and policy staffing, and their directors became in effect deputy mayors (and sometimes more than that)."[6]

As shown in Table 3.2, the data on Model Cities lend some support to the proposition that the length of a community's prior experience in program development is positively related to the success of its service-coordination efforts. The findings here indicate a moderate-positive association (gamma .331) between length of prior experience and success of coordination.

There is no empirical evidence in the literature that directly addresses the questions of whether the ethnic composition of target areas for service-coordination projects will influence the degree to which coordination efforts are successful. Theoretically, a case can be made for anticipating an inverse relationship between the percent of racial minorities in the target area and the success of coordination efforts based on a number of assumptions. For example, fewer participating agencies would be inclined to get involved in programs concentrating on predominantly minority neighborhoods because of the citizen participation requirements of the Model Cities Program. These requirements meant that, for the agencies involved, minority residents would not only be clients whom these agencies serve but they would also become members of the agencies' input constituency—a prospect that many agencies might find uncomfortable to countenance. Secondly, in minority neighborhoods, resident ambitions to control the program were expressed more forcefully than in majority neighborhoods.[7] And this ambition, though not often realized, might have discouraged local agency involvement in the program.[8] Finally, in pro-

Table 3.2
Planning Experience and Success in Coordination
(in percent)

	Prior Experience in Urban Renewal		
Degree of Success	Low	Medium	High
Low	36.4	11.8	19.0
Moderate	59.1	64.7	61.9
High	4.5	23.5	19.0
	100	100	99.9*
	(N=22)	(N=17)	(N=21)

*Due to rounding.

Notes: gamma .331; X^2 = 5.447; Df = 4; N.S.

grams serving predominantly minority neighborhoods it was often desirable for staff to be minority-group members. These programs may have had to settle for less-experienced and less-professional personnel than programs in predominantly white neighborhoods because of the limited pool of experienced minority professionals from which they had to draw.

The findings on the relationship between racial composition of the target area and coordination success in the Model Cities Program are equivocal. As indicated in Table 3.3, the data suggest that there is a weak inverse association (gamma −.218) between these variables. This finding is equivocal because the data also reveal that while low ratings of coordination success are rarely associated with predominantly white target areas, high success of coordination ratings occurred as frequently in predominantly minority target areas as in target areas with few minority residents.

COMMUNITY PLANNING PROCESSES

For all communities participating in the Model Cities Program, approximately one year of planning preceded efforts to implement projects in a coordinated service system. At the conclusion of the Model Cities planning year, the CDAs submitted a Comprehensive Demonstration Plan to the Department of Housing and Urban Development. In order to prepare these plans, cities first had to set up a planning structure—an organizational system by which to gather and exchange information in order to make decisions that could be agreed upon by the several parties involved in the proposed service-coordina-

Table 3.3
Ethnicity of Target Area and Success in Coordination
(in percent)

Degree of Success	Minority Composition of Target Area		
	Less than 40 percent	40-74 percent	75+ percent
Low	6.7	28.6	28.6
Moderate	73.3	71.4	52.4
High	20.0	0	19.0
	100	100	100
	(N=15)	(N=14)	(N=21)

Notes: gamma −.218; X^2 = 5.786; Df = 4; N.S.

tion efforts. Much of the work of the CDA during this planning period was devoted to creating the action system that produced the local plan. By statute, that action system was required to be composed of local residents, service agencies, and CDA staff. The arrangements varied in terms of the number and size of policy-making groups, involvement and support of the local chief executives, and the amount of influence exerted by citizen groups in the planning process. These variations make it difficult to conceptualize the planning process along a single dimension. Thus, in analyzing the relationship between planning processes and the implementation of service-coordination projects we examine the following four variables that characterize different aspects of these planning processes: support of the chief executive, degree of citizen influence in planning, structure of citizen participation, and the degree of conflict in the planning period.

Chief Executive Support

Success in planning for the coordination of services requires that planners obtain agreement about the allocation and exchange of resources among diverse and, often, competing interest groups. This requires not only technical and administrative skills but also the sanction and power to mediate and, if necessary, to override competing claims when an impasse occurs. The local chief executive would appear to be one prominent source for sanctioning planning and implementation of service-coordination projects. In her study of city planning agencies Rabinovitz observes:

> Since the 1940's there has been a pronounced trend away from the independent planning commission and toward agencies within the municipal bureaucracy. This change was probably spurred by theories showing that the executive structure provided a compelling answer to the problems of implementing city plans. The theories indicated that . . . plans not having political support are likely to be ineffectual.[9]

While local chief executives were not directly engaged in the daily business of Model Cities planning, they had the responsibility of guiding, mediating, and exercising final authority over the program. The extent to which they fulfilled this responsibility varied.

Findings in the literature concerning mayoral influence and its impact on program development suggest the following proposition: The degree of chief executive support for the Model Cities Program will be directly associated with the success of planning for and implementation of coordination projects. While evidence from the literature in support of this proposition is strong, it is not entirely one-sided. For example, in the Introduction to his analysis of mayoral influence in urban policy making, Kuo notes that many studies tend to present the mayor as "a political actor of limited power" responding mainly to the dictates of business groups or to pressures from other powerful groups in the community.[10] Kuo's findings run contrary to this weak-mayor hypothesis, however. The results of his study, based on data collected from 93 cities, indicate that the adoption of community programs was directly related to the degree of mayoral support they received.[11] Similarly, Rosenthal and Crain, in a survey of 1,186 cities, found that local chief executive support was a major factor in the outcome of decisions concerning fluoridation.[12] Finally, and closer to the subject, data in support of the proposition are found in a Department of Health, Education, and Welfare study of the integration of services in 30 projects. The results of this study indicate that one of the most important factors facilitating services integration was "support from the external socio-political environment in which the project functioned. . . ."[13]

The findings from Model Cities are in the expected direction (gamma .214) as shown in Table 3.4, though the relationship between chief executive support during the planning period and implementation of coordination is not as strong or as conclusive as we might have expected based on the literature.

Looking at the impact of chief executive support during the planning period from another perspective, we find a much stronger relationship (gamma .534) between this variable and the percent of categorical funds in the Comprehensive Demonstration Plan (CDP). As we shall note in Chapter 4, the percent of categorical funds in the CDP is used as an indicator of the degree of financial commitment obtained from agencies that planned to participate in and support coordination projects. This finding suggests that the strongest and most direct

Table 3.4
Chief Executive Support in the Planning Period
and Success in Coordination
(in percent)

| Degree of Success | Chief Executive Support | | |
	Weak	Moderate	Strong
Low	20.0	45.0	0
Moderate	60.0	45.0	84.6
High	20.0	10.0	15.4
	100	100	100
	(N=10)	(N=20)	(N=13)

Notes: gamma .214; X^2 = 8.946; Df = 4; p < .10.

impact of chief executive support during the planning period was upon assembling resources and securing commitments of funds from agencies in the interorganizational field rather than upon the implementation of coordination efforts which took place the following year.

While many agencies might be willing to negotiate with the CDA in the anticipation of obtaining some part of the supplemental funds that the CDA would receive from HUD, getting these agencies to commit categorical monies to the Model Cities projects was a more difficult matter. Categorical funds were obtained, almost exclusively, from federal agencies that have regional, state, and local subdivisions or counterparts. Almost invariably, one or more of the subdivisions or counterparts of the agency below the federal level must approve and support a project that receives categorical funds. Therefore, the task of obtaining funds from an agency at the federal level required that the CDA be able to negotiate relationships with at least one other subdivision or counterpart of that agency at another level. The fact that the compliance of the local counterpart of the federal agency was necessary in order to receive categorical funds gave the local agencies a major point of leverage on the CDA.*

In approaching agencies on these matters, CDA staff could appeal to their sense of higher purpose, emphasizing the professional values of rational planning and coordination of service-delivery projects. Or the case could be made for committing categorical funds to the Model Cities enterprise on the basis of enlightened self-interest. But the logic and persuasiveness of these efforts notwithstanding, the presence of vigorous support from the local chief executive appears to have had a substantial influence on the CDA's capacity to secure categorical funds from agencies, as indicated in Table 3.5.[15]

The behavior of the chief executive appears to be related also to the percent of *local* funds in the CDP budget. Percent of local funds is an indicator of generalized local political support for the coordination program rather than an indicator of agency support, because local contributions were most likely to be reckoned as part of the overall city budget. Therefore, as we shall note later, percent local is less directly associated with degree of coordination success than percent categorical. However, like percent categorical, the percent of the CDP budget composed of local contributions bears a moderate-positive association to the degree of chief executive commitment (gamma .395). This is an additional example of the importance of the chief executive's role in helping the coordination agency acquire needed resources.

---

*However, the CDA had counterleverage because, in most cases, supplemental funds could be used to pay the local share of program costs that is required for most federal categorical programs. This was a peculiar feature of the Model Cities Program that has been carried over to some of the recent special revenue-sharing programs. The significance of this funding arrangement is illustrated by the fact that in one study of 48 categorically funded Model Cities projects it was found that approximately two-thirds used supplemental funds as the local share.[14]

Table 3.5
Chief Executive Support for Model Cities Program
and Percent Categorical Funds in CDP
(in percent)

Percent Categorical Funds in the CDP	*Chief Executive Support for Model Cities Program*		
	Weak	Moderate	Strong
Low (0-12%)	64.3	31.4	21.1
Medium (13-32%)	28.6	40.0	21.1
High (33+ %)	7.1	28.6	57.9
	100	100	100
	(N=14)	(N=35)	(N=19)

Notes: gamma .534; X^2 = 12.755; Df = 4; p < .02.

Citizen Influence

There are a number of reasons given in the literature for involving members of the target area population in the decision-making process related to the creation of coordination projects. One of the main reasons is that they can be instrumental to the planning process and help in the development of meaningful plans.[16] As Bloomberg and Rosenstock explain, residents "can contribute much from their own experience to the formulation of programs and projects to alleviate poverty."[17] A similar view is included in HUD's explanation of the specific assumptions upon which performance standards for citizen involvement in the Model Cities Program were based: ". . . the best intentioned officials and technicians are often by their training, experience, and life styles unfamiliar with or even insensitive to the problems and aspirations of model neighborhood residents; therefore resident ideas and priorities can result in more relevant, sensitive, and effective plans and programs."[18]

However, there is another side to the assertion that those who have experienced the problems of living in low-income communities have a special insight into their situation that can enhance planning efforts. That is, people adjust where possible. For a variety of reasons residents of low-income neighborhoods may be less objective in assessing their circumstances than professional planners. There is some empirical evidence to suggest that such residents tend to be less critical of their environments than professional planners.[19]

Another major reason for active citizen involvement in planning is that, whether or not it improves the quality of the planning product, citizen participation is instrumental to the implementation of plans. That is, citizen participation is necessary because without it the effectiveness of implementation would suffer. But it is by no means clear as to how much citizen influence in the planning process is required if such participation is to serve the objective of paving the way for implementation. Does attainment of this objective require, for example, more than an advisory type of participation? A definitive answer to these questions cannot be given. But evidence from Rossi and Dentler's study of citizen participation in urban renewal suggests that commitment to implementation can be achieved through a passive form of citizen participation in which little policy-making influence is exercised in the development of the plan. As they indicate:

> Reviewing the successes and failures of the citizen participation activities of the Conference, it is clear that this organization made its greatest contribution in its passive rather than its active roles. That is to say, the Conference obtained for the idea of planning and for the plan itself a mass base of support which facilitated the planning process and the acceptance of the Final Plan in the local community and "downtown." At the same time, however, the Conference was unable to modify the plan to conform in all details to the goals the Conference held out as desirable.[20]

Having raised a few questions about the extent to which strong citizen influence in planning is a necessary prerequisite to the successful implementation of service-coordination projects, let us now turn to examine the results in

Table 3.6
Citizen Influence in Planning and Success in Coordination
(in percent)

	Citizen Influence		
Degree of Success	Weak	Moderate	Strong
Low	34.1	—	20.0
Moderate	52.3	69.2	70.0
High	13.6	30.8	10.0
	100	100	100
	(N=44)	(N=13)	(N=10)

Notes: gamma .357; X^2 = 7.596; Df = 4; N.S.

Model Cities. As shown in Table 3.6, there appears to be a moderate positive association (gamma .357) between the degree of citizen influence in planning and the implementation of coordination. However, examination of the distribution within the cells of Table 3.6 indicates that there is more of a curvilinear than a linear relationship. That is, more of the communities in which citizen influence was at either the weak or the strong end of the continuum received low ratings on their implementation of coordination than received high ratings. Communities where citizen influence was moderate received proportionately more high ratings on coordination than communities where citizen influence was either weak or strong. None of these communities where influence was moderate received low ratings on coordination, and almost one-third were rated in the high-degree-of-coordination-success category.

A similar pattern of relationships is found with regard to success in securing commitments of categorical funds from agencies. As indicated in Table 3.7, more of the communities in which there was moderate citizen influence in the planning process had high percentages of commitments of categorical funds from agencies than communities in which citizen influence was either weak or strong.

There is a low-negative association between the percent of local contribution to the CDP budget and citizen influence (gamma −.161). That is, where citizen influence in the CDA was strong, the percentages of local contributions were more likely to be lower than in other communities. On this measure, the CDAs with weak citizen influence are more likely to come out with higher percentages of local contributions than others, whereas CDAs with moderate citizen influence are more likely to come out with higher percentages of categorical funds than others. The reason for this, we believe, is that the staff-

Table 3.7
Citizen Influence and Percent of Categorical Funds in the CDP
(in percent)

Percent of Categorical Funds in the CDP	Citizen Influence		
	Weak	Moderate	Strong
Low (0-12%)	33.3	21.4	60.0
Medium (13-32%)	42.4	21.4	6.7
High (33+ %)	24.2	57.1	33.3
	100	100	100
	(N=66)	(N=28)	(N=15)

Notes: gamma .126; X^2 = 16.776; Df = 4; p < .001.

dominant CDA (where there was weak citizen influence) was more likely to be run as an instrument of the city's executive office; therefore, they were more likely to be supported as one of the city departments. The parity CDAs (where there was moderate citizen influence) were somewhat more independent and served more of an integrating function among the agencies, citizens, and city government. They were, therefore, more likely to be working actively and cooperatively with the agencies from which categorical funds were obtained.

These findings are supported, in part, by another study of funding patterns in the Model Cities Program in which it was observed that citizen-dominated CDAs, in particular

> were often reluctant to work through the established agencies although such agencies were the only legally eligible applicants for categorical funds. . . . With categorical funds the contractual relationships would be between the Federal government and the grantee agency, with the CDA, at best, having a possible veto over the grant by refusing to "sign-off." This desire to retain control sometimes led the CDA to forego the use of categorical funding in favor of supplementally funded projects run by neighborhood groups and new non-profit corporations. The desire for local control also tended to keep the CDA and the eligible applicant agency from working together to obtain categorical funds.[21]

This finding implies that citizen influence in planning is of instrumental value to the implementation of service-coordination projects, provided that it is not overbearing. The finding does not, however, inform us as to precisely what it is about the pattern of moderate citizen influence that, presumably, facilitates the achievement of implementation. Is it the blending of technical expertise with the values and knowledge of local residents? Is it the commitments to implementation that are developed through meaningful citizen involvement in planning? The data do not answer these questions. And we can only speculate that perhaps both of these factors played a role in the achievement of a successful coordination record in those communities where a moderate degree of citizen influence was incorporated in the planning process. But, having entered the realm of speculation, let us offer another explanation that transcends these factors.

It might be observed that these findings are a rediscovery of the golden mean between technocracy and democracy. Or that they support the well-worn advice that "moderation is best." Both observations may be correct in a sense, but they should not be taken literally to mean that a moderate amount of citizen influence is instrumentally the best device for the achievement of planning objectives. Rather, it may be that we are dealing here with a more subtle characteristic of communities which we could describe as a general capacity to achieve the golden mean; this capacity to modulate the inputs of citizens, agencies, and professional planners, we think, is what accounts for variations among cities in achievement of coordination objectives. In planning, as in other human affairs, to find and cultivate the golden mean requires patience, discipline, and skill. That this holds true for the Model Cities enterprise should be apparent immediately to anyone who has engaged in planning efforts that involve creating a structure and process for residents, agencies, and city hall to communicate and exchange ideas around the design of policy for service-coordination projects.

Cooperation and trust among parties are essential to the development of parity in planning arrangements, as is the tolerance of a certain amount of ambiguity concerning the locus of "final authority" and how and when it may be exercised. The sophisticated use of bargaining, negotiation, and willingness to compromise before the brink are also important in sustaining parity arrangements. That is to say, to create and maintain parity planning arrangements requires a constellation of social and political skills and attitudes on the part of residents and professionals that is not characteristically found in communities where CDA staff dominated decision making to the exclusion of citizen influence or where staff abdicated most decision-making powers to citizen groups. Hence, the parity communities' high ratings on coordination may be as much a reflection of the planning skills and expertise available in those communities as of the instrumental value of citizen influence per se. Theoretically, this explanation would account, at least in part, for the weaker ratings on coordination and categorical funding that were associated with both staff-dominant and citizen-dominant planning arrangements.

Structure of Citizen Participation and Degree of MNA Conflict

Staffing links between official coordinating agencies such as CDAs and citizen participants are considered important factors associated with the development of citizen influence. Professional opinion and empirical evidence support the proposition that when resident organizations have the authority to hire their own staff they can operate independently of the official planning and coordinating agency; with this kind of arrangement, strong citizen influence is more likely to develop than when staff are assigned to resident organizations at the discretion of the coordinating agency.[22] At the same time, when strong citizen influence is exercised through an independent residents' organization, the CDA's ability to coordinate is likely to suffer. Sundquist and Davis's investigation of 16 Model Cities indicates some of the difficulties that arise when an independent citizens' organization exercises control over the planning process:

> In cities where the CDAs have become resident-dominated, the plans sent to Washington lack something in the degree of official commitment to them;

heads of city agencies that were left out of the planning process regard
themselves as less than fully bound. And agencies outside the city government, that may be difficult to harness into a concerted effort even with the
mayor's active leadership, have even less attachment to the process.[23]

In examining this aspect of the planning process we used the following classification to identify the structure of relationships between CDAs and citizen
organizations:

1. CDA hired and assigned staff that worked with residents' organizations.
2. CDA hired and assigned staff that worked with residents based on recommendations of the residents' organizations.
3. The residents' organization hired and paid its own staff who were independent of the CDA.

These three arrangements constitute a continuum in regard to the pattern
of CDA-resident-organization relationships according to the degree to which
resident-organization staff were controlled by the coordinating agency. As
shown in Table 3.8, there is moderate negative relationship (gamma −.389)
between success in the coordination effort and citizen control of staff working
with resident organizations. In communities where resident organizations con-
tracted directly for their own staff there were no cases in which coordination
efforts were judged to be highly successful, compared to 21.7 percent of highly
successful ratings given to communities in which the coordinating agency had

Table 3.8
Residents' Organization Staff Autonomy
and Success in Coordination
(in percent)

	Resident Organization Staff Autonomy		
Degree of Success	Low (hired by CDA)	Moderate (hired by CDA based on citizen selection)	High (hired by resident organization)
Low	17.4	20.0	28.6
Moderate	60.9	70.0	71.4
High	21.7 / 100	10.0 / 100	0 / 100
	(N=23)	(N=10	(N=14)

Notes: gamma −.389; X^2 = 3.997; Df = 4; N.S.

major authority in selection and assignment of staff to the residents' organization.

In communities where resident-organization staff is not under the direct control of the CDA, the planning process is probably marked by less cooperation and more of an adversary relationship between citizens and the CDA than in communities where resident-organization staff are personnel of the CDA. This relationship is evident in the association between the degree of conflict experienced in development of the citizen participation structure and degree of autonomy of resident-organization staff (gamma .383).

Resident organizations with independent staffs are likely to exercise forceful influence in the planning process. The adversary type of relationship and the forceful influence of resident organizations may create a sociopolitical climate that is inimical to coordination. A primary reason for this is that the agencies that are potential participants in the coordination effort may hesitate to commit themselves to the enterprise until there is clarification and stabilization of CDA-resident-organization relationships. It appears, however, that agency commitment is inhibited not so much by the general turbulence associated with struggles for citizen influence as by the prospect of entering into a relationship with a CDA that may be dominated by an independent citizens' organization. This is suggested by the fact that, contrary to expectation, we found no substantial relationship (gamma .078) between degree of success in coordination and degree of conflict per se experienced in the development of the citizen participation structure.

NOTES

1. For a sample of studies where community size is analyzed in relation to planning and policy outcomes see Terry Clark, "Community Structure, Decision-Making, Budget Expenditures and Urban Renewal in 51 American Communities," *American Sociological Review* 33 (August 1968): 576–93; Terry Clark, "Urban Typologies and Political Outputs: Causal Models Using Discrete Variables and Orthogonal Factors, or Precise Distortion Versus Model Muddling," *Social Science Information* 9 (December 1970): 7–33; Robert K. Yin et al., *Citizen Organizations: Increasing Client Control over Organizations* (Santa Monica: Rand Corp., 1973), pp. 50–51; Neil Gilbert, Harry Specht, and Charlane Brown, "Demographic Correlates of Citizen Participation: An Analysis of Race, Community Size, and Citizen Influence," *Social Service Review* 48 (December 1974): 517–30.

2. Thomas Dye, "Urban School Segregation: A Comparative Analysis," *Urban Affairs Quarterly* 4 (December 1968): 141–65.

3. Michael Aiken and Robert R. Alford, "Community Structure and Innovation: The Case of Urban Renewal," *American Sociological Review* 35 (August 1970): 650–64; and Michael Aiken and Robert R. Alford, "Community Structure and Innovation: The Case of Public Housing," *American Political Science Review* 64 (September 1970): 843–63.

4. Aiken and Alford, "Community Structure and Innovation: The Case of Urban Renewal," op. cit., p. 662.

5. Aiken and Alford, "Community Structure and Innovation: The Case of Public Housing," op. cit., p. 863.

6. James Q. Wilson, "The Mayors vs. The Cities," *The Public Interest* 23 (Summer 1969): 30.

7. For example, see Melvin Mogulof, "Coalition to Adversary: Citizen Participation in Three Federal Programs," *Journal of the American Institute of Planners* 35 (July 1969).

8. The relative degree to which resident control in minority neighborhoods was actually realized is analyzed in Neil Gilbert, Harry Specht, and Charlane Brown, op. cit.

9. Francine Rabinovitz, *City Politics and Planning* (New York: Atherton Press, 1969), p. 40.

10. Wen H. Kuo, "Mayoral Influence in Urban Policy Making," *American Journal of Sociology* 79 (November 1973): 620. In support of the weak-mayor hypothesis, Kuo cites studies by Floyd Hunter, *Community Power Structure* (Chapel Hill: University of North Carolina Press, 1953) and Peter H. Rossi, "The Organizational Structure of an American Community," in *Complex Organizations,* ed. Amitai Etzioni (New York: Holt, Rinehart, and Winston, 1965).

11. Kuo, *op. cit.,* p. 637.

12. Donald Rosenthal and Robert Crain, "Executive Leadership and Community Innovation," *Urban Affairs Quarterly* 1 (March 1966): 39–57.

13. U.S. Department of Health, Education, and Welfare, *Integration of Human Services in HEW: An Evaluation of Service Integration Projects,* I (Washington, D.C.: Government Printing Office, 1972), p. 46.

14. U.S. Department of Housing and Urban Development, *The Federal Grant Process: An Analysis of the Use of Supplemental and Categorical Funds in the Model Cities Program* (Washington, D.C.: Government Printing Office, 1972), p. 9.

15. For further discussion of the implications of mayoral support for coordination in Model Cities see James Sundquist and David W. Davis, *Making Federalism Work: A Study of Program Coordination at the Community Level* (Washington, D.C.: The Brookings Institution, 1969), pp. 110–16.

16. There is certainly evidence that professional planners do not always develop programs and provide services that are meaningful and appropriate to the needs of inner-city residents. For an excellent example see Herbert Gans, *The Urban Villagers* (New York: The Free Press, 1962).

17. Warner Bloomberg, Jr., and Florence W. Rosenstock, "Who Can Activate the Poor: One Assessment of 'Maximum Feasible Participation'," in *Power, Poverty and Urban Policy,* eds. Warner Bloomberg, Jr., and Henry J. Schmandt (Beverly Hills: Sage Publications, 1968), p. 316.

18. U.S. Department of Housing and Urban Development, *Citizen Organizations: Model Cities Management Series Bulletin No. 6* (Washington, D.C.: Government Printing Office, 1971), p. 3.

19. For example, see Neil Gilbert and Joseph Eaton, "Who Speaks for the Poor: Research Report," *Journal of the American Institute of Planners* 34 (November 1970): 411–16; and Charles Grosser, "Middle Class Professionals . . . Lower Class Clients" (Ph.D. diss. proposal, Columbia University, 1963).

20. Peter Rossi and Robert Dentler, *The Politics of Urban Renewal* (New York: The Free Press, 1969), p. 286.

21. U. S. Department of Housing and Urban Development, *The Federal Grant Process,* p. 15.

22. For opinions and evidence on this proposition see Sherry Arnstein, "A Ladder of Citizen Participation," *Journal of the American Institute of Planners* 35 (July 1969): 221–22; Roland Warren, "Model Cities First Round: Politics, Planning and Participation," *Journal of the American Institute of Planners* 35 (July 1969): 247; James Sundquist et al., op. cit.; and Robert Yin et al., op. cit., p. 59.

23. James Sundquist et al., op. cit., pp. 99–100.

CHAPTER

4

ORGANIZATIONAL CHARACTERISTICS

INTRODUCTION

Knowledge about relationships between organizational characteristics and degree of success in coordination of services is sparse and tentative. In the literature there are more questions and theories on this topic than empirical evidence to guide the effective management of coordination efforts.

The theoretical literature dealing with the interorganizational field provides a framework for viewing the organizational and political problems that coordination projects must address. It is a commonplace observation in studies of the interorganizational field that in order to survive, an organization must establish cooperative relationships and exchanges with other elements in its environment. These "other elements" are variously defined. For example, they are conceptualized broadly by Warren in terms of "input constituencies" (that is, groups that perform supporting functions and to whom the organization is accountable) and "output constituencies" (that is, the target groups or consumers of the organization's services).[1] Similarly, Dill identifies those parts of the environment upon which an organization's goal achievement is potentially dependent as: clients or customers; suppliers of needed resources such as funds, staff, and equipment; competitors; and regulatory groups. Taken together, these elements constitute what he calls the "task environment."[2] An organization's claim to its sphere of activity, purpose, and objectives is substantiated through interaction with the task environment. Thompson sums it up as follows:

> The establishment of domain cannot be arbitrary, unilateral action. Only if the organization's claims to domain are recognized by those who can provide the necessary support, by the task environment, can a domain be operational.

31

The relationship between an organization and its task environment is essentially one of exchange, and unless the organization is judged by those in contact with it as offering something desirable, it will not receive the inputs necessary for survival.[3]

Applying these observations to coordination efforts in the Model Cities Program, we can anticipate that organizations staking out broad claims to do comprehensive planning and coordination (such as the CDA) will have unsettling effects on the interorganizational field. That is, the Model Cities Program involved numerous organizations whose activities and objectives were concerned with the enhancement of social welfare. Before the arrival of Model Cities, these organizations will have achieved a consensus about which activities will be kept in each organizational domain. The Model Cities Program and the CDAs add a new element to the interorganizational field which disrupts the existing consensus. This is similar to the development described in Rose's study of the Community Action Program:

When a new organization brings with it an unclear set of domain expectations, regulations insisting on new participants in the local game, and undetermined methods of organizational interaction, the domain consensus within the community is unsettled. This was clearly the case with the Community Action Program. . . . The comprehensive thrust of the anti-poverty effort involved itself immediately in the domain concerns of every service system.[4]

While the intrusion of the CDA, a new coordinating agency, may pose a threat to the existing domain consensus in the interorganizational field, it also presents an opportunity to obtain new federal funds (the supplemental grants from HUD). In this sense there was a basis for exchange because the CDA had something to offer agencies in return for their involvement in Model Cities projects, for their recognition of the CDA's coordinative role, and, most important, for their support in obtaining commitments of federal categorical funds for specific programs. Whether or not an agency participated in a coordination effort depended, in part, upon how the cost of this exchange was perceived in terms of the agency's autonomy and, in part, upon whether the agency's input constituency favored the proposed coordinative arrangement. As indicated in the last chapter, where local political leadership (a major input constituency of many community agencies) supported the Model Cities Program, the CDA was able to acquire larger commitments of categorical funds than in communities where political support was not strong.

In this chapter we examine some of the characteristics of the organizational systems that developed from the Model Cities coordination experiences. The analysis is divided into two sections. In the first section we will present an overview—the large picture of the organizational map—by identifying the types of agencies, their levels of commitment, major federal sources of categorical funding, and regional variations in agency participation and categorical funding. In the second section we will analyze the extent to which the factors of numbers of agencies in the program, degree of agency financial commitment, and size of the coordinating body are associated with degree of success in the implementation of coordination.

OVERVIEW

Types of Agencies and Levels of Involvement

The frequency with which different types of agencies were involved in some aspect of Model Cities planning and coordination is shown in Table 4.1. Based on reports from 112 Model Cities, the first column of numbers in the table indicates the numbers of cities in which each of these types of organizations played a role in the planning process; agreed to a formal program role in the Comprehensive Demonstration Plan; and/or played an active role in program implementation during the first action year. As the data reveal, the most frequent participants were public agencies—boards of education, departments of health, probation/correction/police agencies, and city planning and recreation departments. The bottom half of the list is composed mainly of private organizations such as churches, family service agencies, colleges, and health and welfare councils which, on the whole, were much less likely to be involved in planning and coordination than public agencies.*

Why were private organizations less likely to participate? Previous discussion of the interorganizational field suggests three reasons that may partially explain this phenomenon. First, some private organizations such as industries, colleges, and chambers of commerce are not typically considered to be within the task environment of social service agencies. Introducing these types of organizations into planning and service-coordination networks probably requires greater effort and more adjustments in the existing domain consensus than is the case with traditional social welfare organizations. Second, political leaders have less leverage with private organizations than with public organizations in which they are important members of the input constituency.

---

*"Social planning department" is the agency type that was reported to participate least frequently by the 112 cities. However, we believe that this is because most city governments do not have this kind of department and it is not a reflection of the degree to which that type of agency participates.

Table 4.1
Types of Agencies' Involvement in Model Cities Planning
and Coordination

Types of Agencies	Number of Cities in Which Type of Agency Participated	Intense Participation– All Aspects of Coordination (percent)	Limited Participation– Planning Aspects of Coordination Only (percent)
Board of education	107	69.2	4.7
Department of health	102	52	19.6
Corrections/probation/police	96	47.9	16.7
City planning	94	42.5	31.9
Recreation	90	50	8.9
Urban renewal	84	52.4	14.3
Department of welfare	83	36.1	36.1
Public employment service	83	33.7	25.3
Public housing	81	32.1	29.6
Office of economic opportunity	81	53.1	18.5
Civic and voluntary agency	72	40.3	29.2
Church	71	31	38
Family service agency	64	35.9	26.6
Chamber of commerce	45	20	37.8
Department of transportation	40	30	42.5
Personnel department	40	35	22.5
Health and welfare council	39	15.4	48.7
Private industry	34	26.5	50
College	29	72.4	10.3
Social planning department	18	33	22.2

Thus, in communities where political leadership strongly supported the Model Cities Program, pressures to participate could be exerted upon public agencies more effectively than upon private agencies. Finally, in getting involved with the CDA, public agencies may have felt their autonomy to be less threatened than private agencies. For private agencies, participation in Model Cities meant that their input constituency would be expanded in varying degrees to include the CDA, local political leadership, and citizen participants. While the private agencies might obtain new funds, in the process they would also become increasingly accountable to these new input constituencies. Generally, public agencies are more accustomed to being accountable to these constituencies.

The levels of participation of different types of agencies, which are listed in the second and third columns of numbers in Table 4.1, suggest that the costs of participation were felt more intensely by private organizations than by public organizations. The second column gives the percentages of each type that participated in all three aspects of the process (that is, intense participation: played role in planning; agreed to a formal program role in the CDP; and played an active role in implementation). The ten types of agencies in the upper part of the table (those with the highest frequencies of participation in the 112 cities, *all* of which are public agencies) have a greater intensity of participation overall than the ten types in the lower part of the table (those with the lowest frequencies of participation, *most* of which are private organizations). The average percentage of intense participation for the first ten types is 48 percent, compared to a 33 percent average of intense participation for the second ten types.

The third column is almost the converse of the second column. These figures show the percentages of each type that participated *only in the planning aspect* of the coordination projects (that is, limited participation). The average percentage of limited participation for the ten types in the upper part of the table is 20 percent, compared to a 34 percent average of limited participation for the second ten types. Thus, not only were private agencies on the whole less likely to participate than public agencies, but the participation of private agencies was more likely to be of a limited nature and they tended to withdraw more often than public agencies after the initial involvement in the planning period.

As previously noted, the lower overall rates of participation for private organizations might be due to the difficulties of involving nontraditional organizations in social planning and to the CDA's relatively weak political leverage with private as compared to public organizations. The higher withdrawal rates of those private agencies that did participate suggests, in addition, that when private organizations actually did get involved and had the opportunity to assess the costs and benefits of participation they may have concluded that the former would be greater than the latter.

Financial Commitments of Government Agencies

The percent of communities in which commitments of categorical funds were obtained from each of the various governmental sources is shown in Table 4.2. According to these data, HEW and HUD were the major contributors of categorical funds in the 112 communities. The third-ranked agency was the Department of Justice, which coincides with the relatively high frequency of participation noted for local correction/probation/police agencies in Table 4.1. Commitments of categorical funds were obtained from each of the other agencies on the list in less than one-third of the participating communities. Of course, in some cases, such as the Department of Agriculture and Department of the Interior, we would anticipate a low degree of financial involvement because of the differences between these agencies' organizational concerns and those of Model Cities.

Regional Variations

To complete the mapping of organizational characteristics of Model Cities planning and coordination efforts we will fill in some of the geographic boundaries within which these efforts took place. There were regional variations among the types of agencies that participated and the degrees of financial commitments that were obtained in Model Cities projects, as revealed in Tables 4.3 and 4.4.

Table 4.2
Sources of Categorical Funds

Organization	Communities in Which Categorical Funds Were Committed in the CDP (percent)
Department of Health, Education, and Welfare	71
Department of Housing and Urban Development	56
Department of Justice (LEAA)	33
Department of Labor	31
State agencies	30
Office of Economic Opportunity	22
Department of Transportation	19
Department of Agriculture	12
Department of Interior	10
Department of Commerce	8
	(N=112)

Table 4.3
Categorical Funding by Region
(in percent)

Categorical Funds in the CDP	1 (North-east)	2 (South-east)	3 (South)	4 (Mid-west)	5 (South-west)	6 (West)
Low (0-12%)	57.1	41.2	15.8	45.0	20.0	20.0
Medium (12-32%)	14.3	35.3	26.3	30.0	46.7	50.0
High (33+%)	28.6	23.5	57.9	25.0	33.3	30.0
	100	100	100	100	100	100
	(N=21)	(N=17)	(N=19)	(N=20)	(N=15)	(N=20)

Notes: $X^2 = 17.921$; Df = 10; $p < .10$.

The data in Table 4.3 report on the percent of categorical funds in the Comprehensive Demonstration Plans by region. These data indicate that communities in the Southern region (Region 3, Atlanta Office) were most likely to secure a high percent of categorical financing, and communities in the Northeastern region (Region 1, New York Office) were most likely to secure a low percent of categorical financing in their CDAs. In general, there appears to be a division among the six regions, with the Southern, Southwestern, and Western regions scoring relatively high on categorical financing in comparison to the Northeastern, Southeastern, and Midwestern regions. This finding may be influenced by the fact that more of the largest cities are clustered in the Southwestern, Northeastern, and Midwestern regions—54 percent of the largest cities, 65 percent of the middle-sized cities, and 35 percent of the smallest cities are in fact located in these regions. A substantial negative association (gamma -.405) was found between city size and the percent of categorical funds in the CDP. This relationship will be explored in greater detail in Chapter 7.

The regional variations in participation by different agencies are shown in Table 4.4. Here the data on agency participation refer only to those agencies that were involved throughout the entire planning and coordination process (intensive participation). Another way to think of these figures is as representing the cases in which CDAs were most successful in involving agencies in Model Cities projects. Generally, the Southern region, which is highest on categorical funding (see Table 4.3), has higher percentages of intensive participation of agencies than the other regions. Also, it is interesting to note that there are higher percentages of intensive involvement of agencies that are, traditionally, least associated with social welfare delivery systems (that is, private industry, chambers of commerce, and colleges), in the Southern, South-

Table 4.4
Agency Participation by Region
(in percent)

Agencies Involved in Three Levels of Participation	Region						Total
	1	2	3	4	5	6	
Board of education	16.2	20.3	24.3	12.2	12.2	14.9	100
Department of health	15.1	17.0	26.4	9.4	17.0	15.1	100
Corrections/probation police	21.7	21.7	19.6	8.7	10.9	17.4	100
City planning	10.0	17.5	22.5	22.5	12.5	15.0	100
Recreation	22.2	17.8	31.1	2.2	13.3	13.3	100
Urban renewal	25.0	22.7	13.6	15.9	11.4	11.4	100
Department of welfare	16.7	10.0	36.7	3.3	16.7	16.7	100
Public employment service	3.6	14.3	25.0	7.1	21.4	28.6	100
Public housing	15.4	23.1	30.8	7.7	19.2	3.8	100
Office of economic opportunity	16.3	16.3	25.6	14.0	9.3	18.6	100
Civic and voluntary agency	31.0	13.8	10.3	10.3	13.8	20.7	100
Church	22.7	13.6	40.9	9.1	13.6	0	100
Family service agency	17.4	13.0	17.4	17.4	26.1	8.7	100
Chamber of commerce	22.2	0	22.2	11.1	33.3	11.1	100
Department of transportation	8.3	16.7	41.7	0	25.0	8.3	100
Personnel department	0	21.4	14.3	35.7	21.4	7.1	100
Health and welfare council	16.7	33.3	33.3	0	16.7	0	100
Private industry	0	22.2	33.3	0	22.2.	22.2	100
College	19.0	14.3	23.8	14.3	4.8	23.8	100
Social planning department	0	16.7	50.0	16.7	16.7	0	100

western, and Western regions (particularly with private industry and chambers of commerce) than the Northeastern, Southeastern, and Midwestern regions. This is interesting because of the probability that there are considerably more colleges and industries in the latter regions. In addition, figures indicate that the Southern region was more likely than any of the other regions to have had churches involved in planning and service-coordination projects.

NUMBERS, COMMITMENTS, SIZE, AND COORDINATION

Number of Agencies Participating in Planning

At first thought, the number of agencies participating in the planning period would seem to reflect the extent to which the CDA actively responded to HUD's requirements for coordination of services. However, it might also reflect the extent to which the planning environment was conducive to agency involvement in the coordination efforts. The data in Table 4.5 indicate an unanticipated and rather important finding about the relationship between number of agencies participating in planning and success of coordination. The data reveal a moderate *inverse* relationship between the number of agencies that were involved in the planning process and the implementation of coordination in the first program year.

This finding can be most easily explained from a practical standpoint; it is relatively more difficult to coordinate activities among many agencies than among few agencies. The meshing of complementary activities and other coordinative tasks are more manageable when fewer than nine agencies are involved with the CDA than in communities where twenty or more agencies are involved. Indeed, whether the coordination of local services can be meaningfully accomplished when the planner must involve the number and scope of services described by HUD as components of a comprehensive approach (see Chapter 1) is dubious.

With what range and mix of services can a coordination project operate most effectively as a mechanism to integrate service delivery? The Model Cities findings suggest that, in terms of numbers, the optimum range of agencies involved in planning is nine or fewer. But numbers alone may not explain the entire story. It would be helpful to understand why communities that were operating under the same set of HUD guidelines and requirements involved different numbers of agencies in planning. One explanation is that city size affects the numbers of agencies available (for example, large cities would have a larger pool of potential agencies to recruit for the coordination effort than small cities). This relationship is analyzed in Chapter 7.

Table 4.5
Number of Agencies Involved in Planning and Success in Coordination
(in percent)

Degree of Success	Number of Agencies		
	Low (fewer than 9)	Moderate (10-15)	High (16-33)
Low	18.7	15.0	35.3
Moderate	56.3	75.0	58.8
High	25.0	10.0	5.9
	100	100	100
	(N=16)	(N=20)	(N=17)

Notes: gamma −.361; X^2 = 4.954; Df = 4; N.S.

Another variable that we would expect to be positively related to the number of agencies participating in planning (assuming equal efforts were devoted to gaining not just participation, but substantive agency commitments to the coordination effort) is the percent of categorical funds in the CDP budget: that is, the greater the number of agencies participating, the more categorical funds potentially available for commitment. However, the data reveal that this relationship is almost negligible (gamma .106). Communities with the fewest agencies involved in the planning process obtained proportionately about as much categorical money as those with the largest number of agencies.* Thus, there appears to be a discrepancy between the quantity of commitments obtained in different communities, as reflected in the number of agencies participating in planning, and the quality of these commitments, as reflected by what participating agencies agreed to contribute to these coordinative arrangements in the form of financial support.

In sum, it is not clear that the inverse relationship found between the number of agencies participating in planning and the success of the coordination effort should be interpreted strictly as a function of the comparatively greater difficulty attributable to coordinating large numbers of participants. At

---

*We should note that the supplemental funds in CDP budgets (against which the percent of categorical funds was calculated) were allocated on a formula basis that was unrelated to the number of participating agencies.

the very least the unanticipated finding that the number of agencies involved in planning had almost no impact upon the percent of categorical funds committed to the program must be taken into account. This suggests that, in addition to a numerical count of agency participation, we must assess the *quality* of agency commitments to the coordination effort (which, in this study, we infer from the percentage of categorical funds in the CDP budget). We will have more to say about agency participation rates when we examine the numbers of agencies that actually participated in the first program year in the next section.

Number of Agencies Participating in Coordination Efforts

Between the planning period and the first program year the number of participating agencies decreased. As noted in Table 4.1, a substantial number of agencies did not participate beyond the planning period. Although, in general, there were fewer agencies participating in the program year than in the planning period, we still find a moderate negative association (gamma -.378) between the number of agencies involved in a project and success of coordination, as shown in Table 4.6. According to these data, projects in which fewer than a dozen agencies were involved were more likely to achieve positive results than those in which there were a larger number of agencies. These data support the following hypothesis, stated by Bolan:

Table 4.6
Number of Agencies Involved in Implementation
and Success in Coordination
(in percent)

Degree of Success	Number of Agencies		
	Low (fewer than 7)	Moderate (8-11)	High (12+)
Low	33.3	23.5	71.4
Moderate	16.7	35.3	28.6
High	50.0	41.2	0
	100	100	100
	(N=12)	(N=34)	(N=7)

Notes: gamma -.378; X^2 = 8.413; Df = 4; p < .10.

If carrying out the proposal involves a great deal of coordination among a large number of autonomous and dispersed groups, it is more likely to be resisted and eventually rejected (largely because of uncertainty that it will actually be carried out as proposed). Even if adopted, it may easily be subverted in implementation. Proposals that concentrate action within a single agency or a relatively few individuals and involve few external coordination problems will more likely be adopted.[5]

We have found no reference in the literature to empirical research on the question of the extent to which numbers of organizations that participate in service-coordination projects affect the degree of success in implementing such projects. However, there is another body of research from which relevant propositions may be drawn. We refer to research on group dynamics, which is relevant to this question because coordination efforts are conducted, in large part, through the work of small groups—the task forces or committees composed of representatives of participating agencies. For example, Thomas found, in a study of welfare departments, that units composed of small numbers of workers achieved greater role consensus than units composed of larger numbers.[6] (While the numbers of workers in sections of welfare departments are different units of analysis than numbers of agencies in coordination projects, the problems of interaction of different numbers of task group members are similar in both cases.)

In another research effort, Hare found that as the size of discussion groups increased, the degree of consensus decreased; members were more dissatisfied with the discussion; there was a tendency for the larger groups to break into factions.[7] These findings suggest some of the difficulties that may have been encountered in the work of committees composed of representatives of a large number of agencies in the Model Cities service-coordination projects.

Our findings in Model Cities, of course, do not suggest that numbers of agencies larger than 12 magically assures the failure of coordination efforts. Rather, the findings underscore a general fact of which planners are aware but which has not received much explicit attention in the studies of service-coordination efforts or in the typical policy guidelines for service-coordination projects. Namely, at some point numbers make a difference: social and physical arrangements for meetings may become burdensome, informal communications may become difficult to sustain, and so forth. Whether the saturation point for the type of coordination projects in Model Cities involves 12, 13, 14, or a larger number of agencies, we cannot ascertain with any precision or confidence. However, our findings suggest that coordination efforts may begin to approach the saturation point within the approximate range of 12 participating agencies.

Financial Commitments and Coordination

While we find that the number of agencies participating in the program is related negatively to coordination, there is a moderate-positive correlation (gamma .296) between the degree of financial commitment of federal funding agencies and coordination ratings, as shown in Table 4.7. The data here indicate that cities with CDP budgets that incorporated a high percent of categorical funds were more likely to achieve high ratings on the implementation of coordination than cities with lower percentages of categorical funding.

One explanation for this finding is that the percent of categorical funds in the CDP may be considered an indicator of the CDA's capacity to mobilize and concentrate resources around Model Cities projects. In this sense the percent of categorical funds reflects a measure of success in efforts to gear up for coordination. And it might be argued that there is a high degree of transferability between the skills and capacity to assemble resources and the ability to move effectively into the next stage—from a state of mobilization to implementation.*

There is a fairly simple explanation for the positive association between percentages of categorical funding and coordination degree of success: there was a higher degree of interdependence between the CDA and participating agencies when there was a commitment by several of the actors to contribute categorical funds to the projects than when these commitments had not been made. As Reid puts it:

> If the presence of coordination is to be accounted for, then perhaps the most general explanation for its occurrence may be found in the notion of organizational interdependence. Two organizations may be said to be interdependent if each organization perceives that its own goals can be achieved most effectively with the assistance of the resources of the other. Interdependent organizations are then drawn into exchanges of resources to serve one another's goals.[8]

---

*There is a low-positive association between percent local funds and degree of coordination success (gamma .167). As we indicated earlier, high percentages of local contributions are more indicative of a CDA's capacity to work with the local executive government than with the agencies (which had local, state, regional, and federal jurisdictions) involved in the coordination effort. Moreover, local contributions constituted a much lower proportion of all CDP budgets than did categorical contributions: in two-thirds of the cities, local contributions were less than 10 percent of the budgets; in three-fourths of the cities, categorical funds constituted more than 12 percent of the budgets.

Table 4.7
Percent of Categorical Funds in the CDP and Success in Coordination
(in percent)

	Percent Categorical Funds		
Degree of Success	Low (0-12%)	Moderate (13%-32%)	High (33%+)
Low	23.8	43.7	0
Moderate	66.7	43.7	81.2
High	9.5	12.5	18.7
	100	99.9*	99.9*
	(N=21)	(N=16)	(N=16)

*due to rounding

Notes: gamma .296; X^2 = 9.166; Df = 4; p < .10.

Size of the Coordinating Agency

The question examined in this section is whether the number of the CDA staff in a coordination project was associated with the achievement of coordination objectives in the first program year. There is a substantial body of literature on the relationships between organizational size and structural/functional variables that suggests different answers to this question. Rothman presents an excellent review and codification of the literature on this topic.[9] Rothman offers the generalization that "the size of an organization does not appear to have a consistent relationship with its innovativeness. Instead, size is important either for or against innovation depending upon other variables that interact with it."[10]

To the extent that the coordination of services is seen as an innovation in the structure and relationships of the interorganizational field, we might infer from this generalization that variations in CDA size will not be strongly associated with success of coordination. Indeed, the proposition that the number of CDA staff is not a critical factor in the outcome of coordination projects is supported by the Model Cities experience. As shown in Table 4.8, the data reveal a negligible degree of association (gamma –.021) between agency size and success of coordination.

A tentative explanation of this finding would consider the potential benefits and costs associated with the operation of a large coordinating agency. On the benefits side, when there are large numbers of staff the CDA has greater

Table 4.8
Numbers of CDA Staff and Success in Coordination
(in percent)

Degree of Success	Numbers of Staff		
	Small (4-18)	Medium (19-29)	Large (30+)
Low	18.5	30.8	20
Moderate	70.4	61.5	60
High	11.1	7.7	20
	100	100	100
	(N=27)	(N=13)	(N=10)

Notes: Gamma $-.021$; $X^2 = 1.54$; Df = 4; N.S.

resources to apply to coordination efforts; they have more manpower to engage other agencies in meetings and discussions around coordination proposals. Yet large CDAs would also tend to have decision-making structures that are more centralized than small CDAs.[11] Compared to CDAs with small numbers of staff, planners in CDAs with many staff members would have less authority and discretion to commit their agencies to formal exchange relationships with other organizations. Hence, on the costs side of the ledger, CDAs with large numbers of staff would require a more complicated process (moving through layers of CDA bureaucracy) to formalize interagency agreements.

NOTES

1. Roland Warren, "The Interaction of Community Decision Organizations: Some Basic Concepts and Needed Research," *Social Service Review* 41 (September 1967).

2. William Dill, "Environment as an Influence on Managerial Autonomy," *Administrative Science Quarterly* 2 (March 1958): 409–43.

3. James D. Thompson, *Organizations in Action* (New York: McGraw-Hill, 1967), p. 28. This slim volume is a rich source of propositions on organizational behavior.

4. Stephen Rose, *The Betrayal of the Poor: The Transformation of Community Action* (Cambridge, Mass: Schenkman Publishing, 1972), p. 164.

5. Richard S. Bolan, "Community Decision Behavior: The Culture of Planning," *Journal of the American Institute of Planners* 35 (September 1969): 307.

6. Edwin J. Thomas, "Role Conceptions and Organizational Size," *American Sociological Review* 20 (February 1959): 30–37.

7. A. Paul Hare, "Interaction and Consensus in Different Sized Groups," in *Group Dynamics: Research and Theory,* eds. Dorwin Cartwright and Alvin Zander (Evanston, Ill.: Row, Peterson and Co., 1953), pp. 507–18.

COORDINATING SOCIAL SERVICES

8. William J. Reid, "Inter-organizational Coordination in Social Welfare: A Theoretical Approach to Analysis and Intervention," in *Readings in Community Organization Practice,* eds. Ralph Kramer and Harry Specht (Englewood Cliffs: Prentice-Hall, 1975), p. 261.

9. See Jack Rothman, *Planning and Organizing for Social Change* (New York: Columbia University Press, 1974).

10. *Ibid.,* p. 468.

11. It should be noted that studies of the relationship between organizational size and centralization of authority have produced contradictory findings. For a review of these studies see Rothman, ibid., pp. 145–47, 470.

5

STAFF CHARACTERISTICS

The directors of Community Development Agencies occupy a central position in the coordination network. That position is the nexus connecting the city's chief executive, CDA staff, policy board, citizens, and community agencies. Although these other actors in the coordination effort have contact with one another, by virtue of his location and authority the CDA director has the greatest opportunity to interact with all of the others. Conversely, because of the location and authority of the CDA director he is the actor most affected by the other actors and by circumstances in the community context.

By "location" we mean that the CDA director is midway between the CDA staff and the chief executive and other policy makers. Moreover, he is —like directors of other agencies involved in the coordination effort—in charge of an agency and he has all of the organizational concerns of any agency director; at the same time he acts as an instrument of the city's political leadership vis-a-vis the other agencies in attempting to realize the objectives of the coordination effort.

The concept of "authority" can assume various meanings. Two of its most common interpretations are: *legal* authority, which refers to those features of a position that provide the incumbent formal powers to control organizational operations (for example, the CDA director had legal authority to hire staff, allocate funds, and assign responsibilities); and *normative* authority, which refers to the exercise of influence on the basis of popular acceptance. Because most CDA directors had approximately the same degree of legal authority we shall be using the term in its normative sense.

Degrees of normative authority exercised by directors varied. In this discussion we shall consider some of the differences among CDA directors and how these differences appear to be related to the outcomes of the coordination efforts. Apart from contextual factors that may influence coordination outcomes—such as community size, previous coordination experiences, and degree of conflict—some of the outcome differences may be explained by variations among the professionals involved in terms of: (1) professional experience, (2) role behaviors, and (3) authority. We can examine one or more dimensions of each of these factors with our data. As we do this we will also occasionally comment upon the apparent effects of contextual factors on staff behavior.

EXPERIENCE: THE CDA DIRECTORS' PROFESSIONAL BACKGROUNDS AND THE CDA STAFF

Our estimate of the CDA directors' experience is derived from their professional positions prior to taking the Model Cities job. Based on descriptions of their prior employment, the directors were categorized as urban-planning specialist (if previously employed as a director of an urban renewal program, for example), human-service specialist (if previously employed as a social worker, for example), or nonspecialist (if previously employed in private industry, for example).

We expected to find that there would be a relationship between the directors' professional backgrounds and degree of success in coordination. That is, CDA directors who were urban-planning specialists, we expected, would bring a higher degree of knowledge and experience to apply to the tasks of planning and implementing a coordination effort. However, our data reveal no distinctive differences in outcomes of coordination efforts associated with the directors' experience. The proportions of CDAs falling into each category of coordination outcome were approximately the same for each category of director experience.

It is interesting to note that the nonspecialist directors were *less* likely to achieve lower ratings on coordination than the others: 27 percent of the urban-planning-specialist directors and 23 percent of human-service-specialist directors were rated low on coordination outcomes compared to only 13 percent of nonspecialist CDAs. The difference is interesting since we had anticipated that the nonspecialists would be more likely than others to achieve poor results because the professional tasks involved in coordinating agencies are exceedingly complex from both a technical and a political viewpoint. A possible explanation for these unanticipated results relates to contextual factors. That is, nonspecialist CDA directors were more likely to be found in cities where the chief executive (the mayor or city manager) was strongly committed to the program. Therefore, the nonspecialist CDA director tended to be working in a context that was politically conducive to the coordination effort. It should be noted, too, that none of the nonspecialist CDA directors achieved high coordination scores; high scores were given to 13 percent and 15 percent of the urban-specialist CDA directors and human-service-specialist CDA directors respectively.

We can conclude little about the effects of CDA directors' experience from these findings. While the effects of experience are equivocal, there is some evidence to suggest that cities are nevertheless more likely to turn to urban-planning specialists for help when their planning objectives encounter difficulties. This supposition is based on the fact that when cities had more than one CDA director during the planning period they were, clearly, most likely to select an urban-planning specialist to replace either a human-service specialist or a nonspecialist.*

As reported in Chapter 4, we find that there is a negligible association between the numbers of CDA staff and coordination outcomes. A second characteristic of the CDA staff that might be expected to affect the outcome of a coordination effort is degree of professionalization. That is, we would anticipate a positive relationship between the professionalization of the CDA staffs and the degree of success in coordination projects because professional knowledge and skill are important resources in planning and implementation of these projects. Our estimate of the degree of staff professionalization is calculated by using the proportion of the total staff of the CDA that has an educational attainment of a college degree or more. While this is a rather gross measure, it does indicate the extent to which CDAs recruited staff members who had formal educational preparation for their positions.

Our data reveal no significant associations between degree of professionalization and coordination outcomes. However, we do not think it is necessary to conclude from this that professionalization makes no difference. Rather, the finding is inconclusive as in the case of directors' professional experience. This finding suggests that contextual and organizational factors may have a more powerful bearing on coordination outcomes than the proportion of CDA staff with at least a college degree.

It is of some interest to note that increases in numbers of staff and increases in degree of professionalization of staff from the planning period to the implementation period were most likely to take place in cities that achieved

---

*The pattern of second selections in 65 cities was as follows:
- 29 percent of the 31 cities that had had urban-planning specialists selected either human-service specialists (13 percent) or nonspecialists (16 percent);
- 78 percent of the 23 cities that had had human-service specialists selected either urban-planning specialists (61 percent) or nonspecialists (17 percent);
- 64 percent of the 11 cities that had had nonspecialists selected either urban-planning specialists (46 percent) or human-service specialists (18 percent).

lower ratings on coordination outcomes. However, in the data used for this observation the numbers of cities in each category are small, and the strength of the associations are low; therefore, this finding can only be considered tentative. It does suggest the possibility that successful coordination projects are less likely than others to expand the size and degree of professionalization of their staffs after the planning period. Less successful coordination projects are more likely to expand their staffs because they are more likely to end up having to do by themselves the work that it was expected would be carried out by the coordinated efforts of several agencies.

SKILL: THE CDA DIRECTORS' ROLE BEHAVIORS

The director of a coordination project must integrate two kinds of activities if he is to attain his objectives: first, he must develop among all of the actors in the coordination project a set of relationships that will facilitate communication, cooperation, and consensus; second, he must bring to the effort some ability to utilize technical procedures and methods. Concern with the first set of activities—development of a set of workable relationships—is a sociopolitical task. These activities include development of an organizational structure in which actors can communicate with each other and work together exchanging ideas and information, solving problems, and mitigating conflicts. The second set of activities—introducing technical procedures and methods—includes data collection (for example, using surveys), specification of problems, ranking priorities, designing programs, and so forth.

In the literature on social planning these two sets of activities are frequently described as distinctive planning perspectives. For example, Rein[1] and Lindblom[2] describe planning as a sociopolitical process, and Kahn[3] describes planning from a techno-methodological perspective. Others [4] have conceived of the planning process as involving both "analytic" (that is, technical) and "interactional" (that is, sociopolitical) aspects that must be integrated even though they frequently strain against one another.

The strain between technical and sociopolitical activities was evident from the beginning of the Model Cities Program.[5] The HUD planning model emphasized the importance of both the sociopolitical and techno-methodological aspects of planning. That is, as much concern was given to achieving widespread participation of area residents, agencies, and political leaders as was given to use of technical expertise in planning. However, HUD guidelines were relatively clear and firm on the techno-methodological side and rather loose and vague on the sociopolitical side. These degrees of specificity regarding analytic as opposed to interactional requirements of planning are not peculiar to the HUD model; they inhere in the nature of the knowledge available about the subject matter. That is, the technical aspects of planning can be described in a concrete, orderly, and step-by-step manner. For example, there are well-established procedures for designing and implementing information-gathering programs such as surveys. The knowledge available about the sociopolitical features of planning is, by comparison, less well developed. For example, the meaning of the term "citizen participation" is vague, slippery, and difficult to specify.

In examining the role behavior of the CDA directors we are interested in the relative emphasis given to the technical versus the interactional activities in the planning period and the implementation period. For simplicity, we will characterize these different role behaviors as task-oriented and process-oriented. Directors are classified on the basis of their responses to the questionnaires completed 1971–72. (This means that most of the 112 directors who responded were reporting after-the-fact and many were reporting on the role behaviors of their predecessors.) Directors classified as task-oriented had selected this kind of item to describe their behavior: "Administered and organized program with strong direction and high expectation of positive and cooperative responses to his leadership from other actors in assigning tasks and developing product components." Directors classified as process-oriented selected different items to describe their behavior: "Usually served as intermediary or service agency for Model Cities actors. Prime function was not substantive but rather provided resources to whomever took leadership."

Our findings indicate that associations between the directors' role behaviors and coordination outcomes are different when we examine the planning-period role behaviors and the implementation-period role behaviors separately. That is, for the planning period there appears to be a very strong association (gamma .827) between the process-oriented role and achievement of high scores on coordination outcomes; this relationship does not hold for the period of implementation where there is a low negative association (gamma –.111) between the process-oriented role and coordination outcomes. The percentages of CDA directors who adopted these different role behaviors in each of the periods and ratings on coordination outcomes are described in Table 5.1. It should be noted that these findings must be considered tentative because the number of cities in which the directors adopted process-oriented roles is rather small in both periods.

These findings become somewhat more interesting when we examine the changes in directors' role behaviors that took place from one period to another. In looking at all 81 of the CDA directors on whom we have role behavior judgments for both periods (Table 5.1 is based on responses from only 39 directors because these are the only ones for which we have both coordination-outcome scores and role-behavior responses), we find that the overall pattern of switching (from the planning period to the implementation period) heavily favored switching to task-oriented roles from process-oriented roles. Only 13 percent of directors who were task-oriented in the planning period switched to process-oriented roles in the implementation period, compared to 48 percent who were process-oriented in the planning period who switched to task-ori-

Table 5.1
Directors' Role Behaviors in Planning Period and Implementation Period by Ratings on Coordination Outcomes
(in percent)

Rating on Coordination Outcomes	Planning Period[a]		Implementation Period[b]	
	Task-Oriented	Process-Oriented	Task-Oriented	Process-Oriented
Low	32	—	24	33
Moderate	59	60	61	50
High	9	40	15	17
	(N=34)	(N=5)	(N=33)	(N=6)

[a]gamma .827; X^2 = 4.923; df = 2; p < .10.
[b]gamma −.111; X^2 = .268; df = 2; N.S.

ented roles in the implementation period. This pattern implies that process-oriented role behavior may be better suited to the tasks of planning for coordination and task-oriented role behavior may be better suited for the tasks of implementing coordination.[6]

By and large, discussions in the literature of planners' role behaviors have turned on questions concerned with the ethics, values, and utility of process-oriented versus task-oriented behaviors.[7] While these questions are relevant for planners, our findings suggest that, in addition, one kind of role orientation is better suited to a particular phase of the coordination project than the other.

In the frequently turbulent, tense, and conflict-ridden context of the Model Cities Programs the emphasis on process orientation in the planning period served the important function of establishing rapport and developing skills. Rothman's statements on the implications of research about the planner's behavior are relevant here:

> In assessing the proper extent of directive role performance, practitioners should take into account the situational context, goals being sought, and attitudes of community participants. . . . Target groups that are distrustful or that feel a sense of distance or inferiority with respect to the practitioner may react negatively to the exercise of more assertive roles; hence, the practitioner should be cautious in regard to assertiveness with such clients and constituencies until trust is established, or disparity in knowledge or skill is reduced.[8]

Once trust is established, skills developed, and planning guidelines agreed upon, the professional's task-oriented activities become more important and gain acceptance. That is, to implement the plan he must create systems for allocating funds to, for reporting on, for evaluating, and for redesigning programs.

There remains, of course, the question of why some of the CDA directors in cities that are judged to be unsuccessful in their coordination efforts appear to shift in the "wrong" direction—from task-oriented role behavior in the planning period to process-oriented role behavior in the implementation period. A tentative interpretation is that in cities where there are poor coordination outcomes the directors either would not or could not engage in process-oriented role behaviors in the planning period. That is, they might have been task-oriented to begin with, or contextual factors may have inhibited their engaging in process-oriented behavior. However, when the planning period terminates and it becomes evident that the coordination effort has failed, these directors may then be more likely to switch to process-oriented behavior. Perhaps the director himself becomes aware of the need to invest more of his energy in sociopolitical role behavior in order to begin to build the system of relationships needed for successful coordination that had not grown in the planning period; or it may be that other elements in the situation change to allow the director to do this.

Our findings on associations between staff role behaviors and coordination outcomes follow the same pattern as those of the CDA directors' role behaviors. For the planning period there is a low-positive association between process orientation of staff and coordination outcomes (gamma .139) and for the implementation period there is a low-negative association between process orientation of staff and coordination outcomes (gamma −.280). Moreover, we find that the shifts from process to task orientations of staff are more likely to take place in cities achieving high scores on coordination than in other cities. These shifts in the direction of the associations between the planning and implementation periods support our findings in regard to the appropriate phasing of the CDA directors' role behaviors. However, here too, the numbers in each category are small and the strengths of the associations are low, so the findings can only be suggestive.

AUTHORITY: CHIEF EXECUTIVE COMMITMENT AND ACCOUNTABILITY TO CITIZENS

In order to achieve successful outcomes in coordination projects the director must have the authority to engage in a large number of complex and delicate interpersonal and interoganizational encounters and exchanges. He cannot deal effectively with executives, professionals, and citizens unless he has the authority to engage in action. (As we indicated earlier, we use the term "authority" in its normative sense because the CDA directors had approximately the same degree of legal authority. Normative authority involves the ability to influence others through informal pressures based on the allocation of symbolic rewards such as "acceptance" and "positive response."[9] CDA directors acquire this authority when they have the commitment of other actors who respect their competence and trust their judgment.)

We would infer, from analysis of our data, that the directors who engaged in process-oriented role behavior in the planning period tended to have higher degrees of normative authority than other directors. This inference is based mainly on the fact that these directors were more likely than others to be in cities where chief executive commitment to the program was rated "active."* The active support and backing of the mayor or city manager lends a certain prestige to the Model Cities Program that would be likely to enhance the CDA director's informal powers of persuasion over other actors in the field. In addition, process-oriented CDA directors were more likely than other CDA directors to hold themselves accountable to citizen participants.† Such accountability opens the door not only for citizens to influence the CDA director's behavior but for the director to establish trusting relationships with citizen groups that would strengthen his ability to bring informal pressures to bear on these groups. (The associations between directors' role behaviors and chief executive commitment are negligible for the implementation period; and the association between process orientation and directors' accountability to citizen participants, which was very strong in the planning period, is considerably reduced in the implementation period.)

SUMMARY

There appears to be no association of any consequence between professional experience and coordination outcomes; cities with nonspecialist CDA directors appear to be less likely than others to achieve lower ratings on coordination outcomes (but none achieved high ratings). However, urban-planning specialists and human-service specialists are more likely to be in cities where there are lower degrees of chief executive commitment. Moreover, when

---

*The gamma measure for chief executive commitment and CDA director process role in the planning period is .427, a moderate-positive association; there is no association between these variables for the implementation period.

†The gamma measure for CDA director process role in the planning period and CDA director accountability to MNA residents is .607, a substantial-positive association; this relationship is reduced to gamma .293 for the implementation period.

there is CDA director turnover (which is associated with turbulence in the planning system) cities are most likely to select urban-planning specialists as replacements for the first CDA directors.

There is a strong association between the process-oriented role behavior of the CDA directors during the planning period and high ratings on coordination outcomes. There is a low-negative association between process-oriented role behavior of the CDA directors during the implementation period and high ratings on coordination outcomes. Overall, most of the changing of role behaviors from the planning period to the implementation period is from process-oriented to task-oriented behavior, and this is more emphatic in cities that achieve high ratings on coordination outcomes. The findings suggest that process-oriented role behavior may be better suited to the tasks of planning for coordination and task-oriented role behavior may be better suited for the tasks of implementing coordination.

Finally, directors who were process-oriented in the planning period were more likely than others to be in communities where there was strong chief executive commitment; and these directors tended to be held accountable to citizen participants.

NOTES

1. Martin Rein, *Social Policy* (New York: Random House, 1970).

2. Charles E. Lindblom, "The Science of 'Muddling Through,'" *Public Administration Review* (Spring 1959).

3. Alfred J. Kahn, *Theory and Practice of Social Planning* (New York: Russell Sage Foundation, 1969).

4. Robert Perlman and Arnold Gurin, *Community Organization and Social Planning* (New York: John Wiley, 1972); Ralph M. Kramer and Harry Specht, *Readings in Community Organization Practice* (Englewood Cliffs: Prentice-Hall, 1975).

5. Neil Gilbert, Armin Rosenkranz, and Harry Specht, "The Dialectics of Social Planning," *Social Work* 18 (March 1973).

6. For a more detailed analysis of the relationship between process-oriented behavior and the planning and implementation phases of program development see Neil Gilbert and Harry Specht, "Process vs. Task in Social Planning," *Social Work* (in press).

7. Irwin Sanders, "Professional Roles in Planned Change," in *Readings in Community Organization Practice,* eds. Ralph M. Kramer and Harry Specht (Englewood Cliffs: Prentice-Hall, 1975), pp. 291–99.

8. Jack Rothman, *Planning and Organizing for Social Change* (New York: Columbia University Press, 1974), p. 75.

9. For a more detailed discussion concerning the exercise of normative power see Amitai Etzioni, *A Comparative Analysis of Complex Organizations* (New York: The Free Press, 1964), pp. 4–10.

6

COORDINATION AND SERVICE DELIVERY

In the preceding chapters we examined factors related to the varying degrees of success achieved by CDAs in their coordination of services during the first program year. Up to this point in our analysis the dependent variable has been the CDAs' degree of success in implementing service-coordination projects. Unstated in the theoretical framework we have been using is the assumption that success in creation of a coherent organizational network within which agency activities are harmonized will produce desirable results. These desirable results involve program implementation—specifically, the effective and efficient delivery of services.

Ideally, an effective delivery system is one in which services are accessible, continuous, comprehensive, and accountable. These outcomes are not necessarily complimentary.[1] For example, an integrated comprehensive delivery system in which channels of communication and referral are highly rationalized (eliminating the duplication and overlap of services) may provide less accessibility and accountability to clients than a delivery system that is fragmented with many overlapping services and many organizational "doors" through which clients may enter the system.[2]

In addition to the effective delivery of services, a well-implemented coordination effort is also assumed to be an efficient service-delivery method. That is, coordinated service-delivery systems that benefit from economies of scale and the elimination of duplications of service are supposed to be less expensive to operate than other service-delivery arrangements. As with the criteria of effectiveness, measures of efficiency are complicated to perform and must include potential costs as well as benefits of the coordinative arrangement. Some of the variables that enter into measures of efficiency are illustrated in the findings of an HEW evaluation of services-integration projects:

It may not be possible to justify services integration strictly in terms of total dollar savings. Centralized/consolidated operation of core services, record-keeping, joint programming, joint funding, joint training, and/or central purchase of service arrangements on behalf of a number of service providers promote economies of scale and coordinated staff utilization, funding, planning and programming, and evaluation help reduce duplication.

Although there are some cost savings resulting from economies of scale and reduction of duplication, they do not appear (at least in the short-run) to equal the input costs of administrative and core service staff required to support integrative efforts. However, if one includes protection of public investment in services as a measure of efficiency, then a stronger case can be made for service integration on grounds of efficiency. If the public investment in one service (job training, for example) is to have lasting benefit only if another service (a job placement service, for example) is also provided, the cost involved in assuring that the client gets the job placement services as well as job training may be justified in terms of protecting the investment in job training.[3]

Of course, the ultimate test of coordinated service-delivery efforts is the quality of the results produced. Are clients served more effectively in the coordinated system than through other service-delivery methods? Is the cost of such service reasonable? There is a dearth of empirical evidence concerning the comparative effectiveness and efficiency of coordinated service-delivery arrangements. This lack of evidence is due in large part to the formidable problems of obtaining qualitative measures of program output. In the absence of qualitative measures of program output, funding agencies must often settle for surrogate measures such as concrete results showing the numbers of programs in operation, numbers of staff delivering services, numbers of clients served, and the like. This was clearly the case in Model Cities. James observes:

'Delivery of services' was a phrase that acquired significance as the program developed. It represented the desire of program managers to show visible accomplishments, and also served as a substitute goal, excusing their failure to achieve others. The mere fact of having delivered a 'service,' regardless of its individual merit or relation to other activities, served the dual function of avoiding focus on other problems and providing a sense of practical accomplishment.[4]

One rough measure of service delivery is the proportion of supplemental funds allocated for the first program year that the CDA was able to spend. As it turned out, spending the money was more difficult than many cities had anticipated. Only one third of the cities that had been operating the program for 12 months were able to spend more than 50 percent of their funds; conversely, two thirds of the cities had spent less than half the funds that had been allocated to them for the first program year. There is evidence that spending performance improves with time because, while the picture of twelve months' spending is bleak, it is a considerable improvement over the picture at six months. That is, at six months, 80 percent of the cities had spent only between 3 to 23 percent of their funds. The comparative rates of spending for six and twelve months are given in Table 6.1.

Federal granting agencies tend to be sensitive about the prompt expenditure of funds within the fiscal year for which they are granted, and this was especially true for Model Cities. Federal officials who must go before Congress to request authorization of funds to solve the cities' problems do not relish the task of explaining why cities could not implement programs and spend the funds they had been granted for the first action year, particularly after so much effort, time, and money had been spent by the cities on program planning. Thus, although spending the money was not an explicit objective of the Model Cities Program, implementation of programs on schedule was certainly desirable. Implementation—the production of concrete results and service delivery —required the expenditure of substantial proportions of the cities' grants. The increased spending pattern for the second six months of the program probably reflects, in part, pressures to accelerate implementation of services that were brought to bear upon the cities by HUD.

Spending patterns as an indicator of service delivery do not tap major substantive aspects of program performance that might be measured along various other dimensions: these indicators do not tell us whether the money was spent wisely. While specific substantive measures of program quality would have been useful, they would have required resources far in excess of those available for our study. And even if measures of the quality of program had been available, the spending criteria would still be required. That is,

Table 6.1
Supplemental Funds Spent by Model Cities
(in percent)

Supplemental Funds Spent	After 6 Months' Expenditures	After 12 Months' Expenditures
10 or less	22	
23 or less	80	
35 or less		32
50 or less	100	67
95 or less		100
	(N=112)	(N=63)

evaluating the overall performance of a program with 10 percent of its projects implemented against the overall performance of a program with 90 percent of its projects in operation would require giving some weight to the proportion of funds spent as an outcome measure.

However, we did obtain general qualitative judgments of overall performance for the first program year as seen from the perspective of HUD officials. The officials interviewed were asked to designate those cities they considered to be "most successful" and "least successful" in regard to overall program achievement. There was substantial agreement between these qualitative judgments and both the percent of supplemental funds spent for 12 months (gamma .459), and success of coordination efforts (gamma .783).

The question that remains is: to what extent was the success of coordination efforts associated with a high rate of service delivery (as reflected in spending patterns)? Theoretically, there is reason to anticipate that the relationship between these variables would not be particularly strong, at least for the first program year covered by our data, because efforts to coordinate service delivery involve negotiating and settling new boundaries in the task environment of participating agencies. Although some of that work may have been accomplished in the planning phase, many of the details of a coordination plan cannot be settled until the individuals and agencies involved begin to implement the plan according to the agreed-upon guidelines. It is often the case that when agencies attempt to implement what was agreed upon in principle they discover many practical problems that had not been anticipated which become the basis for disagreement and delay. The staff of the coordinating agency needs to establish relationships with the staff of the agencies participating in the program. Questions of supervision, professional status alignments, and responsibility for scheduling meetings and setting agendas must be settled.[5] And the interorganizational strains that develop as participating agencies strive to balance their involvement in the coordination enterprise with their desire to retain their autonomy in their particular service-delivery domain must be resolved. In all, putting the new sets of relationships into operation in the coordination process is a time-consuming effort. As noted in the HEW evaluation of service-coordination projects:

> The study indicates that service integration is an evolutionary process. It takes time for service integration to occur—time for organization and implementation of a project, time for a project to attain legitimacy in the eyes of service providers, and time for participating agencies to develop a comfortable working relationship, often a necessary prerequisite to the coordination or consolidation of agencies' functions.[6]

Given that coordination of service delivery is an evolutionary process, we might reasonably expect that where agencies became seriously involved in this process the cities would not exceed in the rate of service delivery for the first program year compared to cities characterized by limited coordination efforts. In the latter cities, it is likely that participating agencies were less occupied with developing interorganizational ties and therefore had more time to go about their primary business of serving clients. One study of the funding process to which we referred earlier suggests that this is the case. They report that "the CDAs that did program their supplemental funds as a match for categorical funds often found their first action year almost finished and only a third to half of their funds spent. Programming of categorical funds created dollar management problems and a bogging down of programs."[7] However, these authors neglect to tell us the comparative spending experiences for other programs.

As shown in Table 6.2, the data lend partial support to the proposition that successful coordination efforts do not produce a high degree of service delivery in the first program year, but also reveal an interesting deviation. As anticipated, the success in implementation of coordination efforts had a weak to negligible degree of association with implementation of service delivery (as measured by spending patterns) for six months (gamma .138) and for twelve months (gamma .080). However, when implementation of service delivery is examined in relation to categorical funding, we find a positive association that increased substantially from the six-month (gamma .211) to the twelve-month (gamma .440) period.

Why was the acquisition of categorical funds in the planning phase so strongly associated with the ability of cities to implement their services rapidly and spend high proportions of their supplemental funds? There are, of course, various possible explanations for this finding. One explanation is that the groundwork for interorganizational relationships was most strongly established in cities where CDAs had worked with participating agencies to acquire commitment of categorical funds for the CDP. Hence, when the program went into operation, agencies in these cities had already settled basic jurisdictional issues and were less hampered by the problems of developing interorganizational relationships while implementing their services than agencies in cities that were unable to secure high proportions of categorical funds.

A second and somewhat related explanation of the association between spending and proportions of categorical funds in the CDP draws on the fact that (as noted in Chapter 3) support of the local chief executive appears to be a primary factor associated with the CDA's capacity to secure categorical funds from participating agencies. When HUD's urgent concerns over the high rates of underspending experienced in the first six months of the program year were conveyed to the Model Cities, we might assume that the same political pressure exercised by the local chief executive to help secure categorical funds was available and used to push for rapid program implementation and expanded service delivery. And, indeed, this is the case. For the first six-month

Table 6.2
Correlations Between Success in Coordination,
Percent Categorical Funds in the CDP,
and Spending Patterns
(in gammas)

Spending Patterns	Coordination	% Categorical Funds in the CDP
Supplemental funds spent at 6 months	.138	.211
Supplemental funds spent at 12 months	.080	.440

spending period we find that there is a negligible-positive association between chief executive commitment and spending (gamma .096). However, for the next six-month period, after HUD put pressure on the cities to implement programs more rapidly, we find a moderate-positive association between chief executive commitment and spending (gamma .455). This is a good demonstration of the importance of the chief executive's role in program implementation.

NOTES

1. For a more detailed discussion of the outcome characteristics of the ideal service-delivery system and their relationships to one another see Neil Gilbert and Harry Specht, *Dimensions of Social Welfare Policy* (Englewood Cliffs: Prentice-Hall, 1974), pp. 107–38.

2. A cogent analysis of the functions of duplication and overlap in organization design is presented by Martin Landau in "Redundancy, Relationality, and the Problem of Duplication and Overlap," *Public Administration Review* 29 (July/August 1969): 346–58.

3. U.S. Department of Health, Education, and Welfare, *Integration of Human Services in HEW: An Evaluation of Service Integration Projects—Executive Summary* (Washington, D.C.: Government Printing Office, 1972), p. 11.

4. Judson E. James, "Federalism and the Model Cities Experiment," paper delivered at the annual meeting of the American Political Science Association, September 1970, Los Angeles, p. 7.

5. For a case analysis of some of the problems that arise as these questions were addressed in a coordination project in the antipoverty program see Neil Gilbert, "Neighborhood Coordinator: Advocate or Middleman," *Social Service Review* 43 (June 1969): 136–44.

6. U.S. Department of Health, Education, and Welfare, *Integration of Human Service Integration Projects*, I (Washington, D.C.: Government Printing Office, 1973), p. 16.

7. U.S. Department of Housing and Urban Development, *The Federal Grant Process: An Analysis of the Use of Supplemental and Categorical Funds in the Model Cities Program* (Washington, D.C.: Government Printing Office, 1972), p. 9.

CHAPTER
7

SUMMARY OF FINDINGS AND
AN EXPLORATION OF
CAUSAL RELATIONSHIPS

A SUMMARY: CHARACTERISTICS ASSOCIATED WITH
ALL-AROUND PERFORMANCE

As a way of summarizing some of the findings of this study, we will attempt to draw together those characteristics of cities that appear to be associated with different coordination outcomes. We have used two different measures to analyze outcomes of the service-coordination projects (degree of success in coordination and service delivery as reflected in spending patterns). By combining these two measures we can apply a somewhat more demanding standard by which to weigh the success of the cities in these coordination efforts. That is, if a city was rated high on *both* of these measures the claim to success is somewhat more persuasive than with high ratings on either of the measures alone; conversely, poor ratings on both measures is a stronger indicator of failure than either rating alone.

Our purpose in combining the ratings is to develop portraits of the best performers (the cities rated high on both measures) and the worst performers (the cities rated low on both measures). The means by which the cities are assigned to the "best" and "worst" categories is shown in Figure 7.1.

There are a total of 42 cities for which ratings on both performance variables were available. Of these 42 cities, 16 (38.1 percent) were in the three cells that were combined for "best" ratings and 17 (40.5 percent) were in the three cells combined for "worst" ratings. As noted in Figure 7.1, cities are in the best category if they are rated high on at least one of the performance variables and medium or high on the other; they are in the worst category if they are rated low on at least one of the performance variables and medium or low on the other.

Figure 7.1
Combined Ratings to Indicate Best and Worst Performance

Service Delivery

		Low	Med	High
	Low	worst	worst	—
Degree of Success	Medium	worst	—	best
	High	—	best	best

The strongest differences between best and worst performers emerge in the 11 characteristics listed in Table 7.1.* We shall describe each category of performers in regard to these characteristics.

BEST PERFORMERS

Cities that achieved high ratings on all-around performance were most likely to be of medium size (50,000 to 249,999).

Although low degree of conflict was the predominant rating for the total population of cities, those cities with medium degrees of conflict are overrepresented among the best. This refers to conflicts expressed around the formation of the citizen participation structure in dealing with such questions as who would have decision-making authority in regard to planning programs and approving the plans, and allocation of planning resources. Best cities were considerably more likely than others to have chief executives with high degrees of commitment to the Model Cities Program. While only 18 percent of the 42 cities had strongly committed chief executives, 40 percent of the best cities had

---

*There are, in addition to these 11 characteristics, four for which we found no differences between "best" and "worst" cities. These were: regional location; CDA directors' role behaviors in the implementation period; racial composition of the MNA; and the number of years of planning experience. In earlier chapters we noted that there was a negligible-negative degree of association between racial composition and coordination outcome and some negligible-positive degrees of association between the other three variables and coordination degree of success. However, as we have noted earlier in this chapter, cities that did well in the process of service coordination did not excel any more than other cities in implementation. Therefore, combining the two outcome measures tends to wash out the rather weak associations that these variables had to degree of coordination success.

Table 7.1
Characteristics Proportionately Overrepresented in Cities Rated Best and Worst for Degree of Success on Coordination and Service Delivery, Combined*

Characteristics	Best (Categories Overrepresented)	Worst (Categories Overrepresented)
Size of population	medium (50,000-249,999)	large (250,000+)
Degree of MNA conflict	medium	high
Degree of chief executive support	high	low
Citizen influence in planning	moderate	weak; strong
Degree of autonomy of resident's organization	moderate	high
CDA director turnover	none	some
CDA director role in planning period	process	task
Number of agencies in planning process	low (1-9)	high (10-33)
Number of agencies in implementation	low (1-7); moderate (8-11)	high (12-31)
Percent categorical funds in CDP	high	moderate; low
Percent local funds in CDP	moderate	low

*To determine proportionately overrepresented categories the following formula was used:

$$\frac{\text{Percent of best (or worst) in a category}}{\text{Percent of the 42 cities in that category}} > 1$$

Where this ratio is smaller than 1, the categories are not shown in Table 7.1. Thus, for example, of the 42 cities on which we have ratings on both performance measures, 40.4 percent were of medium population size, but of the 16 cities that achieved "best ratings" 56 percent were medium sized. Accordingly, medium-sized cities are proportionately overrepresented among the best performers. The large cities represented 31 percent of the total; but 47.1 percent of the 17 cities rated worst were in the large-city category. Thus, large cities are proportionately overrepresented among the worst performers. Small cities are not reported on in Table 6.3 because they were not proportionately overrepresented in either the best or the worst rated cities.

such executives, more than two times the number that would occur if the chief executive ratings were proportionately distributed among the cities.

Generally, citizen influence was most likely to be weak in the total population of cities (66.7 percent had weak citizen-influence systems). However, 31.2 percent of best cities had moderate degrees of citizen influence in planning. Similarly, resident organizations with moderate degrees of autonomy were infrequent, occurring in only 19.2 percent of the total. But moderation was much more frequent among the best cities: 40 percent had such arrangements, two times the proportion that could be expected if the ratings were evenly distributed.

CDA director turnover was slightly less frequent in the best cities than in other cities. That is, proportionately fewer of them had more than one director, though the difference is small. The directors' role behaviors in the planning period were task-oriented in the majority of cities (83.3 percent). However, in 33.3 percent of the best cities the directors' role behaviors were process-oriented, two times the amount that could be expected if role behaviors were proportionately distributed.

The number of agencies participating in planning and implementation of the coordination program were most likely to be low in the best cities. And, finally, the majority of best cities had high proportions of categorical funds in their CDP budgets. Although only 24.1 percent of all cities had high percentages of budgeted categorical funds, 69.2 percent of the best cities had high percentages, more than two times what might be expected proportionately. Best cities were more likely to have moderate percentages of local funds in their CDP budgets and they were underrepresented among those cities with low percentages.

WORST PERFORMERS

Cities with "worst" ratings on all-around performance were most likely to be of large size (250,000+ population) and to have experienced high degrees of conflict. None of the worst cities had chief executives with high degrees of commitment to the Model Cities Program and they are overrepresented by low degrees of chief executive commitment.

Worst cities are markedly underrepresented in moderate citizen-influence systems and overrepresented by both weak and strong resident-influence systems. These cities were likely to develop patterns of planning in which either staff or residents were dominant. Worst cities are also overrepresented by resident organizations with high degrees of autonomy.

CDA director turnover was somewhat more likely to occur in worst cities, although the difference is not very large. Task-oriented CDA director role behavior, which occurred in most of the total of cities (83.3 percent) was even more likely to occur in worst cities (90 percent).

Numbers of agencies participating in planning and implementation of the coordination program were most likely to be high in these cities. And, finally, worst cities are overrepresented among those with low and moderate percentages of categorical funds in their CDP budgets, and they are overrepresented among those with low percentages of local funds in their CDP budgets.

Thus far in this report, we have found that there are a number of interrelated variables that are associated with degree of success in coordination. It is rather difficult, dealing with only one set of relationships at a time, to keep track of the ways in which these variables interact. Although we have controlled for intervening variables at different points in the analysis, it is difficult for the reader to follow a discussion in which a series of variables are successively controlled for one another. Moreover, it is difficult, using this mode of analysis, to determine the weight that should be given to these different variables. Thus, in our portraits of the best and worst cities, we cannot say which of the differences are most important.

However, if we control for the effects of several variables at one time we will be able to compare the relative importance of the factors bearing upon services coordination that we have been discussing up to this point. Ordinarily, one would not attempt to test hypotheses by path analysis with the limited number of cases involved in this study. However, we have gone about as far as we can go with these data in testing hypotheses; therefore, in the next section we shall present some exploratory models of the coordination process by using multivariate analysis.

AN EXPLORATORY MODEL OF CAUSAL RELATIONSHIPS IN THE COORDINATION PROCESS

Our intent in this section is to develop some hypotheses about the causal relationships among selected variables we have dealt with in Chapters 3 to 6. The purpose is to construct an exploratory model of relationships among variables using multiple regression analysis. By this means we can identify what appear to be the significant causal relationships when each of several variables in the model is held constant in relation to each of the others. The n's with which we are working in this analysis are rather small for testing hypotheses with these statistical techniques. However, we believe that the effort will yield some useful hypotheses for subsequent research. Based on the findings in the previous chapters, eight variables were selected to form an initial model that might explain the relationships among community characteristics, organizational characteristics, and the degree of coordination success. In that model we have eliminated considerations of staff characteristics. While there is some evidence in Chapter 5 to support our interpretations of the relationship between CDA directors' role behaviors and coordination outcomes, the distribution of values on staff characteristics is highly skewed so that these data cannot be used in the regression analysis. We also altered our original framework in regard to degree of citizen influence and degree of autonomy of resident-organization staff. Based on the analysis in Chapter 3, it seems to us to be more sensible to treat these two variables as organizational characteristics rather than contextual variables because they both appear to be influenced by contextual factors such as degree of conflict in the MNA.

The structure of the initial model is presented in Figure 7.2. Theoretically, the assumptions underlying this model are that community characteristics (for example, executive commitment) have an impact upon the type of organizational arrangements that develop (for example, categorical funds committed and staff autonomy); and it is also assumed that these community characteristics and organizational arrangements influence coordination outcomes. For purposes of a preliminary assessment, Pearson Product-Moment Correlation Coefficients were calculated to examine the relationships among all the variables in the model as shown in Table 7.2. It can be seen from the varying strengths of these correlation coefficients that several of the potential paths in the model can be eliminated on the basis of the weakness of the associations.

Since the hypothesized causal relationships are in one direction, one-tailed t tests were done to assess the significance of path coefficients. Relationships that are not significant at a .10 level or better and where the predictor variable did not lead to a significant increment in the explained variance were eliminated from the model. The model in Figure 7.3 is based on the significant causal relationships among community characteristics, organizational arrangements, and coordination outcomes. The predictors in the model explain 21 percent of the variance in degree of coordination success.

Table 7.2
Pearson Product-Moment Correlation Coefficients for Variables
in the Degree of Coordination Success Model

	1	2	3	4	5	6	7	8
1. Executive commitment	–	–	–	–	–	–	–	–
2. Planning experience	-.158	–	–	–	–	–	–	–
3. Size	-.096	-.118	–	–	–	–	–	–
4. Categorical funds	.390	-.177	-.224	–	–	–	–	–
5. Staff autonomy	-.241	.148	.243	-.117	–	–	–	–
6. No. agencies in implementation	.074	-.118	.229	.145	.036	–	–	–
7. Citizen influence	.021	.316	-.025	.095	.205	-.100	–	–
8. Coordination success	.121	.166	-.139	.197	-.245	-.324	1.56	–

FIGURE 7.2

Predictors of Degree of Coordination Success

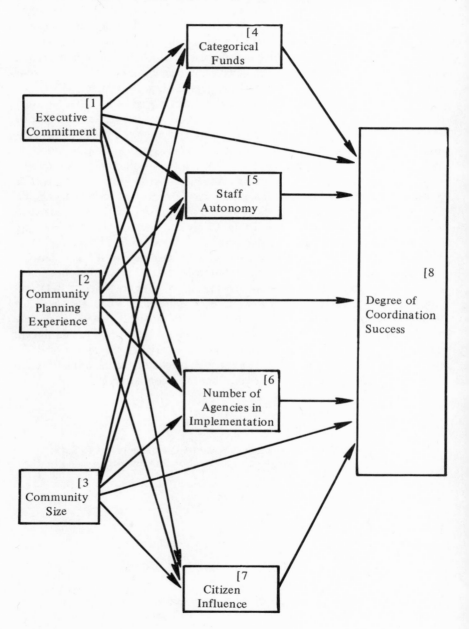

Figure 7.3
Path Analysis Describing Causal Relations among Community Characteristics, Organizational Arrangement, and Coordination Outcomes

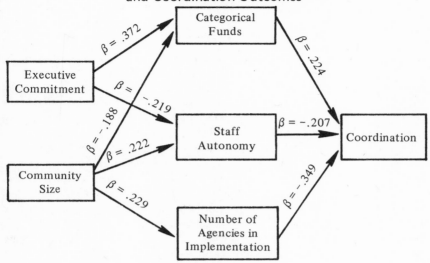

Of the three community characteristics in the initial model, community planning experience was eliminated. When path coefficients in the new reduced regression model are calculated, we find that executive commitment and community size have a significant causal relation to two of the organizational variables (categorical funds and staff autonomy). Community size is also related to number of agencies in implementation.

The community characteristics do *not* have direct causal paths to coordination outcomes. Rather, it is the organizational variables categorical funds, staff autonomy, and number of agencies in implementation that have causal relationships with coordination outcomes. Citizen influence was eliminated as a causal variable using the above-stated criteria.*

The meaning of this model of causal relationships as an explanation of coordination outcomes is that community characteristics affect coordination primarily through their influence upon the organizational arrangements that develop. Chief executive commitment has a positive effect on categorical funds and depresses the degree of resident-organization staff autonomy; the effects of community size are exactly the opposite: size has a negative effect on categorical funds and a positive relationship to staff autonomy. In addition,

---

*Previous findings suggest a curvilinear relationship between citizen influence and coordination outcomes.

size has a positive effect on the number of agencies in implementation. Thus, chief executive commitment tends to influence organizational variables in ways that increase their positive effects on coordination while community size influences organizational variables in ways that decrease their positive effects on coordination.

CAUSAL FACTORS IN DEGREE OF SERVICE DELIVERY

The reader may recall that in Chapter 6 we found only a negligible association between degree of success in coordination and degree of service delivery (gamma .138 at six months and .080 at twelve months). This·finding appeared to us to be justified theoretically in terms of other research findings, and from a practical point of view of the realities of community planning. However, we also indicated in Chapter 6 that degree of success in service delivery (as measured by spending patterns) was strongly associated (at twelve months) with percent of categorical funds in the CDP budget (gamma .440) and we suggested that this might be accounted for, in part, by the preceding factor, executive commitment, which influences positively percent categorical. While executive commitment has a positive relationship to percent categorical, we also found that the other major contextual variable, community size, is negatively related to percent categorical.

Thus, with these associations in mind, our initial conception of the causal paths of the variables that affect degree of success in service delivery is presented in Figure 7.4. A number of variables had already been eliminated as significant in the regression analyses for coordination outcomes so that this initial model is relatively simpler than the model described in Figure 7.2. The Pearson Product-Moment Correlations (See Table 7.3) indicate that all three independent variables (executive commitment, community size, and categorical funds) have better than a .30 correlation with spending.

The model described in Figure 7.5 is based on the significant causal relationships among community characteristics, coordination outcomes, and

Table 7.3
Pearson Product-Moment Correlation Coefficients
for Variables in the Degree of Success
in Implementation Model

	1	2	3	4
1. Executive commitment	—	—	—	—
2. Community size	-.096	—	—	—
3. Categorical funds	.390	-.224	—	—
4. Spending	.334	-.393	.304	—

implementation outcomes that emerge by use of regression analysis. As before, one-tailed t tests were used to assess the significance of path coefficients. Relationships not significant at a .10 level or better are discarded and new path coefficients calculated. The predictors in the model explain 24 percent of the variance in degree of success in service delivery.

Figure 7.4
Initial Conception of Causal Paths of Variables Affecting Spending

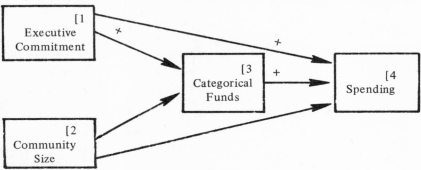

Figure 7.5
Path Analysis Describing Causal Relationships among
Community Characteristics, Categorical Funds,
and Degree of Implementation Success

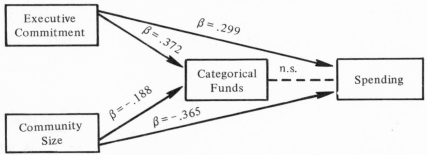

The model in Figure 7.5 suggests that there is not a causal path between categorical funds and spending. Rather, there is a direct causal (positive) link between executive commitment and both categorical funds and spending; and a direct causal (negative) link between community size and both categorical funds and spending. It is interesting to note that the zero order correlation between categorical funds and spending (.304) is significantly reduced (.130, N.S.) when we control for chief executive commitment in this model. Another interesting feature of these relationships is that when we take account of the joint operation of these variables we are led to conclude that the positive effects of executive commitment on categorical funds and the negative effects of community size on spending are somewhat more important than we originally thought. Clearly, chief executive commitment is the strongest determinant (a positive one) of categorical funding and community size is the strongest (negative) determinant of spending.

CONCLUSION

The models of the coordination process that we have described support some of the theoretical and practical propositions we have discussed throughout this analysis. Success in coordination is more likely to occur when there are strong commitments from participating agencies, when the number of participating agencies is kept small, and when participating citizen organizations do not operate with extremely high degrees of autonomy. Chief executive commitment is the factor that is most likely to produce these organizational characteristics and to enhance the capacity of the community to implement the coordination effort. Large community size is the factor that works against the organizational characteristics that enhance coordination and service delivery.

8

IMPLICATIONS FOR PRACTICE

What practical insights do the Model Cities experiences have to offer that might inform other efforts to coordinate social services? In this final chapter we will attempt to cull the implications for practice suggested by some of the study's main findings on the relationships among community context, organizational factors, staff characteristics, and success of coordination.

COMMUNITY CONTEXT

The findings indicate that coordination efforts are likely to be most successful in medium-sized cities (100,000–140,000). A characteristic of small cities that probably reduces chances for successful coordination is their relative lack of professional expertise and experience in planning; a characteristic of large cities that is likely to impede coordination efforts is the complexity of interorganizational relationships that one finds in communities where there are many huge bureaucratic agencies.

While practitioners obviously cannot change city size, an awareness of the obstacles to coordination posed by large and small cities suggests certain corrective measures that might be taken. For example, in small cities efforts could be made to increase the available pool of professional expertise and experience. However, it must be recognized that apart from the fact that small communities cannot afford to support too many full-time professional employees, many professionals prefer to work in larger, more cosmopolitan communities. Therefore, the smaller community finds it more difficult than others to attract skilled and seasoned professionals.

An alternative way of increasing the pool of expertise is to engage professional consultants; most of this work is done by private consulting firms and a small part of it by academics from colleges and universities.* When this alternative is used, however, the community with insufficient professional expertise will be somewhat disadvantaged in dealing with professional consultants. The political and professional leaders of the community are more likely to be both insecure and uninformed in their dealings with professional consultants and, therefore, less likely to be able to establish appropriate contracts with them.

Federal agencies could provide more assistance to small communities in dealing with such relationships. Given that they are used so extensively, federal agencies could provide guidelines for selection of firms, model contracts, referral services, and advice to agencies in their dealings with consulting firms.

A different corrective measure seems called for in large cities. Here the disruptive effects of complexity could be reduced by limiting the size and scope of the coordinating effort. Our data show that degree of success in coordination is related negatively to the numbers of agencies engaged in the coordination project: the greater the number of agencies the less likely it is that the project will be successful. Large cities have larger numbers of agencies; ergo, it is more possible to have large numbers of agencies participating in the larger cities. Planners in large cities should, therefore, make special efforts to limit the numbers of agencies participating in coordination projects. We should note, too, that success in implementation (that is, *spending the money*) of coordination projects is also related negatively to the numbers of agencies participating. That is, more large cities had difficulty in *spending the money,* which we have found is related to size.

Finally, city size is positively related to the degree of autonomy of the organization of residents (who were the consumers in the case of the Model Cities). However, extreme degrees of resident-organization staff autonomy were found to be negatively associated with success of coordination. Cities in which there were intermediate degrees of resident-organization staff autonomy were the most likely to have successful coordination outcomes.

Of course, in the large cities there are more likely to be large subpopulations that form special interest groups based on shared characteristics such as race, class, and neighborhood; these groups are more likely than residents' groups in smaller and more homogeneous communities to claim autonomy. In the long run, the benefits of extreme degrees of autonomy of the consumers' organization appear to be dubious, whereas the benefits of consumer organizations having intermediate degrees of autonomy are considerably higher.

---

*Approximately 70 percent of the Model Cities made use of professional consulting firms. A somewhat larger proportion of small cities made use of them than others did.

The data reveal a moderate positive relationship between a city's prior experience in urban development programs and success in coordination. With experience in social planning, cities develop a capacity for responding to new programs. This most likely occurs because of the accumulation of knowledge and experience by political and professional leaders and members of community organizations. Communities in which there has been relatively little experience in planning social programs are relatively disadvantaged in competing for categorical funds, particularly in programs like Model Cities which require a high degree of integration of political, organizational, and technical skills. Funding agencies should take this into account when assessing the comparative worth of program plans submitted by cities. The city with relatively little experience cannot be expected to have as great a planning capacity as the city with many years of experience. In addition, as previously noted, the funding agency might find programmatic ways to provide extra planning support to less-experienced cities.

On the scene in the less-experienced city, the social planner would be well advised to "go slow," keeping program objectives adjusted to the community's capacity. There apparently is something learned and accumulated from experience; the time and energy that are invested over several years in developing professional leadership pays off.

The strongest and most direct impact of chief executive support during planning was in helping the coordinating agencies (CDAs) secure commitments of funds from other agencies. These financial exchanges served to confirm proposed interorganizational relationships and to facilitate the implementation of coordination efforts.

Chief executive support, it appears to us, is one of the primary factors determining the outcome of coordination efforts. The planner should invest heavily in the cultivation of that support. The chief executive's concern and knowledge about a program will be essential in eliciting the cooperation and aid of department heads and executive staff in other governmental and voluntary agencies. Other kinds of support (for example, of residents) are not a suitable substitute for chief executive support. In communities in which there are high degrees of conflict and in which resident organizations dominate the planning process, the chief executive tends to give only moderate or weak support to the program. In those situations the chief executive perceives that he has little control over the planning process. However, where he believes he can integrate a service-coordination program into his overall approach to city governance he is more likely to work for it.

The findings show that communities in which there were moderate degrees of citizen influence in planning were more likely to be successful in the implementation of service coordination projects than communities in which citizen influence was either very weak or very strong. It is not clear to what extent this finding reflects a special contribution of citizen input to planning for coordination. It is possible that the finding reflects a more general constellation of social and political skills on the part of residents and professionals that contribute to both a balanced degree of citizenship involvement in planning and successful implementation of coordination. The findings do suggest, however, that practitioners should aim for a planning arrangement in which residents (or consumers), political leaders, and professional experts work together, each with a clear understanding of the rights and responsibilities of the others. Coordination efforts will be hampered in communities where professionals and politicians feel no responsibility to listen and respond to powerless consumers or where irate consumers become so incensed with government that they harass and intimidate local officials to the point of preventing them from carrying out their functions.

As with citizen influence, a moderate degree of resident-organization staff autonomy appears to be associated with successful coordination efforts. It is no simple matter to achieve this objective. In recent years consumers have begun to strive for increased autonomy and authority in their relationships with service-providing agencies. Faced with demands for increasing the autonomy of consumers in the planning system, the planner might encourage expansion of the central policy-making body to include more consumers. Consumers who achieve these new positions in policy making are likely, themselves, to resist awarding extreme degrees of policy-making autonomy to an independent organization of consumers.

ORGANIZATIONAL CHARACTERISTICS

The most frequent participants in the coordination projects were public agencies—boards of education, departments of health, probation/correction/-police agencies, city planning agencies, and recreation departments. Voluntary organizations such as churches, family service agencies, colleges, and health and welfare councils were, on the whole, much less likely to be involved in the planning and coordination efforts than public agencies. Moreover, when they did participate, public agencies participated with greater intensity than the private organizations, which were much more likely than public agencies to withdraw after an initial involvement in planning.

Planners, therefore, should court the prospective voluntary organization participant with some degree of caution and should be prepared to invest the amount of time and energy that will be required for adjustments in the existing domain consensus when some private organizations not traditionally associated with social welfare are engaged in coordination efforts. Furthermore, a sensitive appraisal of the private organization's willingness and capacity to deal with new constituencies, along with, perhaps, some anticipatory training in this matter to let the agencies know what they can expect in terms of new constituent pressures, would serve the interests of both coordinative bodies and potential private agency participants. Any effort that is invested in a careful "sounding out" of the extent to which the voluntary agency's interest and capacity for participation are genuine would appear to be worthwhile.

The Southern region achieved the highest degrees of intensive involvement of agencies that are, traditionally, least associated with public social welfare delivery systems (such as private industry and colleges). This finding is interesting because although there are more churches in the Southern region, there are considerably more colleges and industries in other regions.

Practitioners should be cognizant of organizational characteristics of coordination projects that might vary with regional settings. The practitioner, of course, has little leverage to change these regional settings, except by moving himself to a different region. However, the finding of the relatively high participation rates in the South of agencies not traditionally associated with social welfare-delivery systems may be useful for increasing the practitioner's awareness of some of the opportunities in that region.

The findings indicate a moderate negative association between number of agencies involved in the planning project and the degree of success in coordination. Between the planning period and the first program year the number of participating agencies in all communities decreased. Although, in general, there were fewer agencies participating in the program year than in the planning period, we still find a moderate negative association between the number of agencies involved in a project and success of coordination. According to our data, projects in which fewer than a dozen agencies were involved in the implementation period were more likely to achieve positive results than those in which there were a larger number of agencies.

These findings do not suggest that involving fewer than 12 agencies will somehow assure the success of coordination projects. Rather, they draw attention to a point that deserves more consideration than is typically given in the development of policy guidelines for service-coordination projects. Namely, there are physical costs and communications costs associated with bringing together representatives of a large number of agencies in service-coordination projects. At some point these costs impede coordination efforts.

Coordinating agencies are frequently under pressures to involve large numbers of agencies in coordination projects. These pressures usually emanate from funding agencies; sometimes, the professionals in the coordinating agency may themselves believe that "bigger is better." However, whatever the source of pressure to involve large numbers, coordinating agencies should resist the "bigger is better" mentality and should weigh the costs of increasing the quantity of agency involvements.

While we find that the number of agencies participating in the program is related negatively to coordination, there is a moderate-positive association between the degree of financial commitment of federal funding agencies and coordination ratings. Our data indicate that cities with CDP budgets that incorporated a high percentage of categorical funds were more likely to achieve high ratings on the implementation of coordination than cities with lower percentages of categorical funding.

The implication for planners of this finding is that they should concentrate effort primarily upon agencies where there appears to be some readiness not only to take but also to commit resources to the coordination project. This exchange of resources creates a high degree of organizational interdependence which cements working relationships between coordinating and participating agencies.

STAFF CHARACTERISTICS

The major findings on staff characteristics concern the ways that professional role behaviors during the planning period and the implementation period seem to influence coordination outcomes. For the planning period there is a very strong positive association between the process-oriented role of CDA directors and achievement of high scores on coordination outcomes; this relationship does not hold for the period of implementation, where there is a low-negative association between process-oriented role and coordination outcomes. Though not as strong, a similar pattern of relationships is found between CDA staff roles and coordination outcomes.

These findings suggest that emphasis on process-oriented behavior (facilitating social relationships in a nonassertive manner) may be more productive in the initial planning phase and emphasis on task-oriented behavior more productive in the implementation phase of coordination projects. Coordination projects seek to change the network of interorganizational relationships. Practitioners should bear in mind that, for all its potential advantages, this change may be perceived as threatening to organizational interests. The phasing of process/task role orientations is one way that practitioners may try to soothe apprehensions associated with coordination projects and to create the interagency agreements and adjustments necessary to move the project forward.

APPENDIX:
QUESTIONNAIRE TO CDA DIRECTORS—
NATIONAL LEAGUE OF CITIES
AND U.S. CONFERENCE OF MAYORS;
MODEL CITIES QUESTIONNAIRE

To the CDA Director: We will appreciate it if the answers to the following questions can be completed as accurately as possible by you or a member of your staff. All information will be treated in confidence and is to be handled only by members of our research staff. Analysis of the data will not mention individual cities but only categories (e.g., small cities/large cities; first round/second round). The data obtained from the questionnaires will be combined with other national data to produce information about the experiences of the Model Cities Program which should be useful to the staff members of CDA's as well as to others who are engaged in urban planning programs. Thank you for your cooperation.

Completed questionnaires should be returned to: Marshall Kaplan, Gans, and Kahn, 560 Pacific Avenue, San Francisco, California 94133, Attn: Sarah Johnson

A. **Name of City:** _____

B. **The CDA Executive Director(s):**
   We want to know about the executive director of the CDA *during the time covered by the planning period and the first program year.* (Some CDA's had more than one executive director in that time period, in which case we want to know about all who served in that position.)

Executive Directors of CDA

	1st CDA Director	2nd CDA Director	3rd CDA Director
Dates of service as CDA Director	From: To:	From: To:	From: To:
Position *before* he became CDA director: *Name of Employer* *Title of Job*			
Major professional identity before taking position as CDA director (e.g. social worker, businessman, lawyer):			
Position *after* he left job as CDA director: *Name of Employer* *Title of Job*			

C. **City Chief Executive** (Note: Where CDA is an agency of another jurisdiction, like a county, please indicate the appropriate official title. Where a city has both an elected mayor and a city manager, indicate the person to whom the CDA director reports.)
   1. Chief executive is (check one): City Manager_____ Elected Mayor_____ Council-Elected Mayor_____ Other (specify) _____
   2. During the time covered by the *planning period and first program year,* did the same person occupy the position of chief executive? yes _____ no _____
   3. If not, please give date(s) on which change(s) occurred: _____

D. **Composition of Model Neighborhood** (Note: If recent changes have occurred, use figures for the planning period.)
   1. Population size of city _____
   2. Population size of Model Neighborhood_____
   3. Percentage of Model Neighborhood population that is Black_____ Caucasian_____Oriental_____Spanish-speaking_____ Native American_____ Other (specify)_____

81

E. CDA Staff

We are interested in the numbers of CDA staff members and their educational backgrounds. Would you indicate the numbers of staff members in each of these categories for the planning period, and then the numbers in each category in the first program year. (Note: Some positions may not have been filled for all or part of the periods. As a rule of thumb, count all staff members who were engaged for at least five months in the period.)

Numbers of CDA Staff in Administrative, Technical Planning, And Community Organization Jobs

	Planning Period	First Program Year
With Advanced Degree Beyond College		
With College Degree		
Some College		
High School Grad or Less		

F. Resident Organization Staff

During the planning period and first program year, which of the following arrangements best describes the relationship to the CDA of the staff members of the resident organization that have administrative, technical planning and community organization functions? (Note: If the arrangement was different in each period, indicate by using "PP" for the arrangement that best describes planning period and "FPY" for first program year.)

1. CDA hires and assigns all staff that works with resident organization _____
2. CDA hires and assigns all staff that works with resident organization based on recommendations of the resident organization _____
3. CDA contracts with another organization to hire and assign staff that works with the resident organization (give names of organization) _____
   _____ _____
4. CDA contracts with resident organization to hire their own staff _____
5. Other (please describe) _____
   _____

G. CDA Director's Role

We want your opinion about the role of the CDA Director in the planning period and the first year of program. Use numbers 1 to 4 giving *1* to the role that *best* describes the central focus of the Director's action in each period and *4* to the role which *least* describes his actions. Numbers *2* and *3* should be placed accordingly. (Note: If there was more than one director in either or both periods, make the judgments for the director who served the most time in that period.)

Director's Role	Planning Period (Rate from 1 to 4)	First Year of Program (Rate from 1 to 4)
1. *Managerial:* Coordinated efforts of various actors and usually was able to achieve unity in definition and implementation of tasks and to produce HUD components on schedule.		
2. *Broker:* Usually served as intermediary, referee, and mediator among actors in defining tasks and product components.		
3. *Directive:* Administered and organized program with		

strong direction and high expectancy of positive and
cooperative response to leadership from most other
actors in assigning tasks and developing product
components.

4. *Secretariat:* Service agent for Model Cities-related
actors. Prime function was not substantive but rather
provided resources to whomever took leadership
and initiative.

H. CDA Staff Role

We want your opinion about the general role behavior of the CDA staff (not
including the Director). Assign *#1* to the role that *best* describes the central focus
of staff behavior in each period and *#4* to that which *least* describes them. Use
#s 2 and *3* accordingly.

Staff Role	Planning Period (Rate from 1 to 4)	First Year Of Program (Rate from 1 to 4)
1. *Facilitators:* Functioned primarily as service person-nel to provide other actors with resources needed to participate in process. Active role in planning process was minimal.		
2. *Brokers:* Major energies devoted to functioning primarily as intermediaries between resident groups and public agencies. Central focus was on achieving consensus among different actors.		
3. *Technicians:* High ability to respond to HUD's process and product requirements with technical skill. Roles were clearly legitimized in view of most other Model Cities actors.		
4. *Technicians/Advocates:* Mixed a high ability to respond to HUD requirements with high degree of responsiveness to resident interests and desire to share decision-making with residents.		

I. Community Agencies and Organizations

We want to know the number and kinds of local private and public community
agencies and organizations which have worked with the CDA. In the following
table, please list those agencies and organizations which played an active role in
planning and implementing the Community Development Program. By "active"
we mean that they had some actual responsibility for carrying out some task, as
distinct from merely lending their names to lists of sponsors and committees.
Using the list of agencies on the left, check any or all of the three columns which
apply. (Note: When you add "others," try to use the generic names of organizations wherever possible rather than local names, e.g., Public Health Dept.,
Chamber of Commerce, "private industrial firm.")

83

Kind of Agency or Organization	**Planning Period** (Played Active Role in Some Aspect of Planning)	**CDP (or CCDP)** (Had a Defined Formal Responsibility for Projects)	**First Year Program** (Assumed Formal Responsibility for Implementing Program or Parts of)
Dept. of Welfare			
Dept. of Health			
Probation			
Corrections			
Police Department			
Recreation			
Health & Welfare Council			
Chamber of Commerce			
Private Industrial Firm			
Board of Education			
Public Housing Authority			
Urban Renewal Agency			
City Planning Department			
Office of Economic Opportunity			
Family Service Agency			
Churches, other religious organizations			
Civic Organizations and Voluntary Associations			
Public Employment Service			
Transportation Dept.			
Personnel Dept.			
Consulting Firm			
Social Planning Dept.			
Others (specify)			

J. **First Year Program Budget**
   1. What was the total budget of the First Year Action Program? $_____
   2. What percent of this budget was composed of (a) Supplemental Funds_____ % (b) Categorical Funds_____% (c) Local Funds_____% (d) Other (specify)_____ %.
   3. Please list the sources of categorical funds: (e.g. Dept. of Labor, HEW, Dept. of Transportation, etc.).

   _____
   _____
   _____

ABOUT THE AUTHORS

NEIL GILBERT is Associate Professor of Social Welfare at the School of Social Welfare, University of California, Berkeley. Prior to joining the faculty he was Director of Research and Planning for the Mayor's Committee on Human Resources, Inc., Pittsburgh, Pennsylvania. In 1975 he studied comparative social security systems while serving as Senior Research Fellow for the United Nations Research Institute for Social Development in Geneva, Switzerland.

Dr. Gilbert is author of *Clients or Constituents* (San Francisco: Jossey Bass, 1970) and co-author with Harry Specht of *Dimensions of Social Welfare Policy* (Englewood Cliffs: Prentice-Hall, 1974). He and Harry Specht have co-edited *The Emergence of Social Work and Social Welfare* (Itasca, Ill.: Peacock Publishers, 1976) and *Introduction to Planning for Social Welfare* (Englewood Cliffs: Prentice-Hall, 1977). Dr. Gilbert's articles have appeared in *Social Problems, Social Work, Social Service Review, Journal of the American Institute of Planners, Public Administration Review, Sociological Review Monographs, Phylon,* and the *Journal of Social Policy.*

Dr. Gilbert holds a B. A. from Brooklyn College and an M.S.W. and Ph.D. from the University of Pittsburgh.

HARRY SPECHT is Professor of Social Welfare at the School of Social Welfare, University of California, Berkeley. Prior to joining the faculty he was Director of the Community Organization Program for Mobilization for Youth, Inc., New York City, and Associate Executive Director for the Contra Costa Council of Community Services. He spent 1974–75 in England as a Fulbright Scholar studying the reorganization of social service delivery systems.

Dr. Specht is co-author with George Brager of *Community Organizing* (New York: Columbia University Press, 1972). He and Anne Vickery co-authored *The Integration of Social Work Practices* (London: Allen and Unwin, 1976), and he and Neil Gilbert wrote *Dimensions of Social Welfare Policy.* He and Ralph Kramer have co-edited *Readings in Community Organization* (Englewood Cliffs: Prentice-Hall, 1969 and 1975) and he and Neil Gilbert co-edited *The Emergence of Social Work and Social Welfare* and *Introduction to Planning for Social Welfare.* Dr. Specht's articles have appeared in *Social Work, Social Service Review, Public Administration Review, Policy and Politics, Journal of Social Policy,* and *Sociological Review Monographs.*

Dr. Specht holds a B.A. from City College of New York, an M.S.S.A. from Western Reserve University, and a Ph.D from Brandeis University.

*COMMUNITY AND REGIONAL PLANNING: Issues in Public Policy, Third Edition

Melvin R. Levin

COMMUNITY ACTION FOR SOCIAL CHANGE: A Casebook of Current Projects

edited by Julian L. Greifer

COMMUNITY DEVELOPMENT STRATEGIES: Case Studies of Major Model Cities

George J. Washnis

POLICY EVALUATION FOR COMMUNITY DEVELOPMENT: Decision Tools for Local Government

Shimon Awerbuch and William A. Wallace

THE SOCIAL IMPACT OF REVENUE SHARING: Planning, Participation, and the Purchase of Service

Paul Terrell, with the assistance of Stan Weisner

*SOCIAL SCIENCE AND PUBLIC POLICY IN THE UNITED STATES

Irving Louis Horowitz and James Everett Katz

SYSTEMATIC URBAN PLANNING

Darwin G. Stuart

URBAN PROBLEMS AND PUBLIC POLICY CHOICES

edited by Joel Bergsman and Howard L. Wiener

—————————

*Also available in paperback as a PSS Student Edition